good
clean
food

super simple plant-based recipes
for every day

---

lily kunin

creator of
CLEAN FOOD DIRTY CITY

---

with a foreword by
BOBBI BROWN

photographs by
GEMMA + ANDREW INGALLS

ABRAMS, NEW YORK

contents

awaken

nourish

beauty from the inside out

by bobbi brown

My obsession with Instagram is right up there with my obsession with eating healthy. My feed is a mix of beauty and fashion images and photos of healthy bowls, smoothies, and salads. It was only a matter of time before I discovered a very cool Instagram account full of beautiful pictures of clean food accompanied by recipes on how to recreate these delicious meals. Clean Food Dirty City quickly became one of my favorites because it had a different take on healthy eating in a busy world—something that I was always trying to master—so I had to meet the woman behind it all.

I started my relationship with Lily over Instagram when she had another full-time job and Clean Food Dirty City was a side passion project. We became fast friends, sharing a love for green juice, kale, and chia seeds, and any gluten-free and dairy-free foods. We both wanted food that makes you feel good and is good for you. I was already sold with her photographs, but then she cooked for me. I was an instant devotee. Lily was one of the first bowl chefs who prepared food that looked as good as it tasted, using only the best ingredients. Her food fueled long days of travel for me, and her cookie dough bites became staples during days on set and at celebrations for my team at the office. It's only natural that her recipes would eventually find themselves within the pages of a book so that everyone can enjoy Lily's good clean food.

When it comes to beauty, I'm a firm believer that it starts from the inside out. For me, it's simple: Your health shows on your face. If you take care of yourself—by eating the healthiest foods possible, drinking a ton of water, and moving your body every day—it shows. You look good and you feel good. You're comfortable and confident in your own skin.

Everyone's journey to health, wellness, and beauty is different. There's no one-size-fits-all answer to feeling and looking good. I always say makeup is about options, not rules. Lily has the same philosophy for food, and this book has all the options you'll ever need to make it your own.

Here's to happy cooking, healthy eating, and having fun.

xo
Bobbi Brown

my story

How are you feeling? Right this second, in this very moment. How about the last week? This is the very first question I often ask my clients. You're probably feeling awesome from that spin class you just crushed or the green juice you had this week. But we're all human. It's inevitable at times to feel off, even *way off*. Truth be told, I wasn't always living a glossy Clean Food Dirty City life. For years, I felt the opposite of great—nearly bedridden with migraines, my body screaming out that something was not right. No number of yoga classes or green juices could keep me from feeling like my head was about to fall off. Nothing changed until I started paying attention to what was at the end of my fork and how it made me feel.

I grew up a food lover. My earliest memories are of planting tomatoes in my garden, picking raspberries at Homestead Farm in Maryland, and plating desserts with my cousin in the back of my uncle's restaurant. My love for trying new foods began at a young age, starting with the smoked salmon, crème fraîche, and caviar amuse-bouche my great-grandmother would always have at holiday gatherings. She was the type of lady who kept truffles in her freezer—I didn't even know what a truffle was—but she had this elegance that mesmerized my eight-year-old self. Little did I know I would be following in her footsteps, first at the same alma mater, and later in the kitchen—only things look a little different and a lot less fancy at my house. One thing we do have in common: I *always* have truffles in my freezer . . . the raw nut, date, and cacao kind!

My story begins with a bump in the road along the way. My life changed when my migraines began. It started with a blinding headache after field hockey practice during sophomore year in high school. The headaches and migraines kept happening, a couple of times a month. I started seeing a neurologist and cycled between doses of strong medicines—some Band-Aiding the migraine symptoms, but most giving me side effects ranging from digestive issues to short-term memory loss.

Fast forward to college. Horrible side effects drove me to swear off all meds, but headaches (and now vertigo) persisted, often coming on stronger than ever. I'd be sitting in class, and out of nowhere it would hit me. The room would start spinning. I prayed the professor would not call on me during one of these spells as I white-knuckled the arms of my chair. I'd retreat to my room every day after lunch, turn off all the lights, and stay in there until my headache subsided the next morning (and then returned by midday). It's a miracle I was able to accomplish anything during that year.

I was sick of feeling sick and sick of everyone asking me why I was always sick. Dozens of desperate web searches later, a little bell went off in my head. I suddenly heard the words of an osteopath I had seen the year prior loud and clear: *I think it could be something you are eating.* We didn't fully explore that route when my blood work all came back clear, no allergies. Could this be?

With nothing to lose, and enough Google evidence to back up my latest experiment, I jumped on the gluten-free train (before there was a bandwagon) the very next day, and the changes were nothing short of a miracle.

Forty-eight hours later, a giant weight had been lifted off my shoulders. I was headache-free. The cloud above my head disappeared, and for the first time since I could remember, I survived a day without that perpetual headache. It was the first moment I made the connection between what I put in my body and how it makes me feel.

While my spirits were lifted in my newfound freedom, I faced a fresh challenge: how to combine my love for delicious food with my need to properly nourish my body. More practically, would it even be possible to avoid gluten on a college campus? My dining hall graciously supplied me with gluten-free pasta and bread, and brown rice wraps (and even a dedicated toaster). And the neighborhood café gladly used the gluten-free bread that I brought in for breakfast sandwiches.

the move

Things were going swimmingly, but a serious dose of reality came postcollege when I arrived in New York City—a place notorious for its energy, excitement, and cramped living spaces—and I was tasked with keeping myself nourished and grounded amid the rush. My early days in the city were spent exploring my West Village neighborhood, acclimating to my first real job, enjoying happy hours with friends, taking yoga classes, and tasting all the gluten-free food I could get my hands on. No wonder it's called the city that never sleeps. In New York, there is always something to do or somewhere to be, and it can feel like the time it takes to grocery shop, cook, and generally take care of yourself is slowly squeezed out of your schedule.

My tiny apartment was not exactly a chef's kitchen. I had a mini stove and about a foot of counter space for prep. Even though my bedroom window looked directly into another apartment and the ceiling of the bathroom once caved in, I adored my place, which was right next door to three friends from college. We made the kitchen work for us.

Monday night dinners became our weekly ritual. We'd pick out a recipe on Sunday and tag team the grocery shopping and cooking. We'd sling grocery bags on our shoulders for the six-flight trek up to their door and joke about how we couldn't do spaghetti squash suppers anymore—squash was way too heavy to carry up there! It became one of my favorite things to do each week—a built-in time to take care of myself, slow down before facing the week head-on, and catch up with great friends over good, nutritious food. We started to add in walks and workouts on the West Side Highway before dinner and homemade honey face masks after dinner. We shared a blender and prepped smoothies to take to work on Tuesday morning.

Meals had to be easy; these small kitchens housed only a couple pots, and I usually had only a few minutes on most weeknights. Most importantly, they had to be bold, flavorful, and delicious. Oh, and make us feel *great*. I figured out how to cut corners in the best way possible—never when it came to the integrity of ingredients or flavor, but how I could use one less ingredient or one less pot, pan, or bowl. I spent time reinventing some of the classics from my childhood like chili, sesame noodles, and minestrone soup. I introduced new classics, such as vibrantly colorful smoothie bowls, lilac-hued chia puddings, and sunny trays of roasted vegetables. I started to feel grounded and at home amid the buzzing energy of New York City.

In my tiny city apartment, the philosophy for Clean Food Dirty City was born.

my food philosophy

Food is one of the great pleasures in life and should be thoroughly enjoyed. Giving up gluten, for me, was not an exercise in restriction but rather a creative endeavor that made me think outside the box and discover foods that were still beyond delicious. I maintain a constant dialogue with my body rather than prescribe to hard-and-fast restrictions.

Everybody is different, and what works for one person (me) might not work the exact same way for someone else (you). I'm a fan of trying to eat organic as much as possible, and sourcing sustainable animal products for the good of the environment and your health, but what you eat is so deeply personal that only you can decide whether adhering to a vegan, raw, paleo, or any other diet feels right. But why use labels? You know yourself better than anyone else.

For me, this shakes out to be a mostly plant-based diet with tons of healthy fats like avocado and nuts, and proteins like lentils and beans. I also incorporate sustainable animal products like ghee, pasture-raised eggs, wild salmon, and responsibly-sourced meat, some of which you will see in this book. It's not a once-a-week or once-a-month type of thing, but rather listening to how my body feels, what it's craving, and what will make it feel its best. One rule: When you are making a shift to a healthier diet, food must taste really, really good. That way you will actually stick to eating healthier! I believe there is still space for indulgences, because at the end of the day, it's not about deprivation; it's about balance.

If you haven't tapped into the intuition of letting how you feel guide what you eat, know that you already have these instincts. What do you crave when you start to feel under the weather? There's a deeply healing soup for you in my "Restore" chapter. Are you dying for a bowl of comfort food? "Nourish" has something for you. Do you need a boost of energy to get you through the afternoon? Turn to the recipes in "Awaken" or "Sustain."

The recipes that follow provide the framework and building blocks for you to make them your own, depending on your preferences. Most are vegan but are adaptable to any type of diet. Don't be scared to make your own modifications. There is plenty of plant-based protein laced throughout these pages, but if your body runs well on lean protein or pasture-raised eggs—go ahead and add them! I encourage you to make these recipes your own, and above all, I hope you feel inspired to listen to your body and decide for yourself how food makes you feel.

10 tips
for living in a
dirty city

(OR ANYWHERE, FOR THAT MATTER)

1. get local

Scope out your local farmers' market or join a Community Supported Agriculture (CSA) program. CSAs provide a way to purchase local, seasonal food directly from a farmer. It's essentially like buying a membership to get the best produce available each month. Having a guaranteed big box of veggies every week helps you stay on track, exposes you to food you might not have discovered, and supports local farmers. Search for a CSA available near you through a national database such as www.localharvest.org/csa.

2. recipe rundown

If you're part of a CSA, look for recipes that feature the ingredients in your box. Otherwise, pick out recipes that include seasonal produce you can grab at your farmers' market or grocery store. I don't plan out every meal because part of city life is unexpected dinners and schedule changes, but even choosing one recipe and having a few things on hand—like chia pudding, a pot of lentils, and grains—suddenly makes a week of meals no problem.

3. make a list, check it twice

Run through the recipes you chose for the week and make a list of all of your missing ingredients. This list helps keep you smart in the kitchen and on budget—if it's not on your shopping list, you probably don't need it! Of course there are exceptions to the rule (like the perfect summer strawberries you can't resist at your farmers' market or a major avocado sale at the grocery store).

4. put it in your calendar

Plan ahead and schedule a few hours each week to cook. Sunday nights are always a great time to make something for the week ahead, and I usually pick one other night when I know I will have more time to prep for the rest of the week.

5. take shortcuts

It's okay to cut corners *sometimes* and definitely okay to make your life easier. Even though it's simple to whip up a pot of beans, there is also a time and a place for canned beans, especially if it means you're going to make chili tonight rather than order pizza or Thai takeout (but there's also a time and a place for that!). Frozen fruit is another one of my favorite hacks for easy smoothies and last-minute snacks.

6. pack your pantry

Stocking up on all the right things will allow you to walk into the kitchen when you seemingly have nothing in the fridge and walk out with a satisfying dinner. This is a skill you can hone over time—some of my favorite recipes have been born in these moments of forced creativity. Check out my pantry section on page 17 to get stocked with the basics.

7. get social

Have friends over for dinner. You'll have much more fun—and be healthier—if you don't feel like a hermit. This lifestyle is not about holing up in your apartment; it's about sharing it with family and friends and cooking together! Check out my Clean Food Dirty City (CFDC) parties for more ideas on page 202.

8. take it down a notch

While eating well is part of being healthy, it's not so great to fixate and obsess about every bite. If you feel overwhelmed transitioning to a healthy lifestyle, do less. Choose one thing that works for you and build from there. It's all about balance, so be kind to yourself and don't stress over the small stuff.

9. make it a meditation

Cooking at home can be completely meditative. This is your time to unplug from your devices and let your nervous system recover from a busy day. Savor the moment and be present. Call me a hippy, but I think food made with loving, calm energy actually tastes better. Feeding this energy into your life will work wonders.

10. have fun

Don't take yourself so seriously when it comes to cooking! Go back time and time again to dishes you love to cook, try new recipes, laugh at kitchen disasters, celebrate kitchen successes, savor a meal you made especially for you, and enjoy dinner around a big table with friends.

the clean food dirty city kitchen

One Saturday night during a freak blizzard, my roommate Sophia and I found ourselves trapped inside the apartment with only one semi-sad head of cauliflower and some arugula in the fridge. We got the cauliflower ready to be roasted, along with some shallots and cloves of garlic, and stuck it in the oven. I put a pot of water on to boil for brown rice pasta, whisked together a lemony dressing, toasted some almonds, and sliced some sun-dried tomatoes. We tossed it all together, added the arugula, and sat down to a meal that was so good it felt as though it was planned!

Last-minute cooking with ease (and delicious results) takes a little planning ahead. This is especially critical on weeknights, when my pantry allows me to whisk up turmeric-tahini dressings, small pots of supergrains, and hearty meals at a moment's notice. No tahini on hand? No worries, I'll substitute some almond butter or soaked cashews or hemp hearts. I promise that once you dive in, you'll feel comfortable making substitutions and getting creative with what you have on hand.

Food isn't the only part of your toolkit—kitchen supplies are also essential, but you don't need thousands of dollars' worth of pots, pans, and blenders. As long as you have the basic tools, you're good to go. If you are truly starting from scratch, it can take a little bit of an investment, but you can do this over time.

KITCHEN ESSENTIALS

Whether you are building your kitchen, updating your equipment, or just trying to figure out what is truly essential (and should get prime real estate in your limited cabinet space), these are the tools, pots, and pans you'll need to almost do it all.

blender

Blenders are one of the most helpful tools to have in the kitchen. There are a number of high-speed ones that are excellent for making delicious smoothies—but they can also make some of the best soups, sauces, and dips. There are other great blenders at lower price points that are also travel-friendly.

food processor

If there is one kitchen tool that can compete with how much I use my blender, it's my food processor. I use it for anything that has more texture like dips, pestos, nut balls, and falafel.

I also love my mini food processor and immersion blender combo. You can use the food processor to make small batches of dressings and sauces, and the immersion blender to puree soups when you don't want to get an extra appliance dirty.

pots and pans

I use two different saucepans in my kitchen, a smaller (2-quart/2-L) one for small batches of grains, and a larger (4-quart/3.8-L) one for brown rice pasta, soba noodles, or steamed vegetables. I also love my heavy-bottomed Le Creuset (it's a 5.5-quart/5.2-L Dutch oven) and my large (8-quart/7.5-L) stockpot, which bubble over with soups and broths all winter long.

Having a stainless steel skillet, as well as a nonstick skillet, will get you through most of your everyday cooking needs. Make sure to choose one with a nontoxic coating. Stainless steel skillets are great for cooking veggies and stir-fries, whereas nonstick skillets excel when you are cooking eggs and tofu. They're foolproof—you don't even have to worry about eggs sticking or tofu crumbling. Purchase pans in the 8-inch (20-cm) to 12-inch (30.5-cm) range, depending on whether you are usually cooking for a couple of people or for a crowd.

baking dishes

As a veg head, investing in a couple of rimmed baking sheets (also called sheet pans) is a no-brainer. Pick out ones that have some weight to them. They are essential for roasting perfect trays of vegetables and baking cookies. If you have space, also pick up a good 8-inch (20-cm) square glass or ceramic baking dish for dishes like lasagna (page 84) and a muffin (or mini muffin) tin for dishes like the carrot gingerbread muffins (page 170).

spiralizer + julienne peeler

I use a spiralizer to make veggie "noodles" and slaws all the time, especially during the summer. My spiralizer of choice is by Inspiralized, and it's great for zucchini noodles. If you're low on storage space, a julienne peeler will shred carrots, summer squash, and zucchini. It's quick and easy to clean (and travel-friendly).

knives

You don't need a whole butcher block of knives; in fact, you can do just about anything with one badass chef's knife. I love my Zwilling 8-inch (20-cm) knife—it has some weight to it and is great for cutting through squash and other hard vegetables. Add a small paring knife and serrated knife to the mix, and you are all set. The key is making sure your knives stay sharp and in good shape—it will keep your fingers safe in the kitchen!

microplane and grater

I use my Microplane for traditional uses like zesting citrus to fold into grains and dressings, but also for grating garlic so it melts into dishes, or shaving fresh nutmeg for crumbles and desserts. Use a grater for vegetables like carrots or zucchini to enjoy them raw in vegetable bowls or to stir into baked goods.

mixing bowls

I love stainless steel, glass, and ceramic mixing bowls. They will get you through just about everything you need to do in the kitchen. One bonus of glass and ceramic bowls: they are pretty enough to serve the salad right out of them so you don't need to dirty another dish.

measuring cups

Pick up a set of measuring cups and spoons as well as a liquid cup measure. Many of the recipes in the book don't require exact measurements, but it's very important when baking and when you are first getting the hang of putting certain dishes, like chia pudding, together.

fine-mesh strainer and nut milk bags

Use your fine-mesh strainer for washing fruit and veggies, draining pastas, lentils, and beans, and even straining nut milk or juices in a pinch. Better yet, for silky-smooth nut milks, grab nut milk bags.

glass containers

Glass containers provide a safe, easy way to store your food in the fridge. You can purchase an inexpensive set at many home goods stores. I also like having some jars on hand to store sauces, dips, and small amounts of leftovers, or to take a smoothie with me on the go.

PANTRY ESSENTIALS

I love to think of this list of pantry items as a pantry make*under*, letting go of the usual clutter of processed foods, dressings, snacks, and cookies, and revealing shelves and drawers that are filled with foods that support your healthiest life. Having these essentials on hand will help you stick with healthy eating, save money, and make delicious meals!

vegetables + herbs

Load up on dark, leafy greens like spinach and kale, cruciferous vegetables, carrots, scallions, basil, and cilantro every week (aka your detox veggies). Dark, leafy greens are major inflammation fighters, support natural detoxification, and are rich in antioxidants and folic acid.

fruits (fresh, frozen + dried)

Keep a few fruits on hand for last-minute snacks and smoothies. Load up on low-glycemic ones like organic blueberries, strawberries, and raspberries. They also freeze especially well, so make sure to have a few bags of them in your freezer at all times. Most dried fruits have a ton of sneaky sugar in them so I have them in moderation. The two main exceptions are goji berries and mulberries. Both are major antioxidant powerhouses and are delicious stirred into granolas and coconut yogurts, or eaten straight from the jar.

citrus

I always have a bag of organic lemons on the counter, along with a few limes. Citrus is my go-to acid in vinaigrettes; a squeeze of citrus juice will brighten up any soup; a sprinkling of zest is great for grain salads or as a topping on chia puddings and fruit salads.

onions, shallots + garlic

Onions, shallots, and garlic (also known as alliums) are rich in antioxidants that reduce inflammation and boost elimination of toxins from the liver. Store them in a cool, dark place.

pasture-raised eggs

Eggs are an excellent source of protein if you aren't following a vegan diet. Pick them up at your local farmers' market. If you're buying from a store, look for eggs labeled "pasture-raised," which, for the most ethical brands, means the egg-laying chickens had real access to roam outdoors.

nuts + seeds (raw, butters, milks, flour)

Nuts and seeds are super versatile—you can snack on them raw, turn them into dreamy butters, blend them into milks, or grind them into flour. I always have almonds, walnuts, cashews, pepita seeds, and sunflower seeds on hand. I use almond meal often, as it is a great flour substitute and used in a few recipes in this book, like the choc-chip cookies (page 193). I also keep a jar of nut milk in the fridge for smoothies, chia puddings, matcha lattes, creamy soups, and more. Check out my tips for making homemade nut milks on page 48.

purified water

Tap water can be filled with chlorine, fluoride, and compound metals. If you aren't able to install a household filtration system—and let's be honest, most of us aren't—use a water filter for all of your drinking water, or find your local purified water store. (Yes, these exist!)

whole grains

I always keep whole grains like quinoa, brown rice, wild rice, and rolled oats on hand. Whole grains can help add sustenance and provide a solid base for meals. Quinoa, although technically a seed, is one of my favorite grains to make at the beginning of the week, since it's great served either hot or cold.

dried and/or canned beans and legumes

Dried beans are a cheap and nutritious option. I also have a few varieties of lentils in the cabinet for last-minute meals along with chickpeas for weekly batches of hummus. While nothing matches home-cooked beans, a few cans of beans are essential for quick dishes like chilies, roasted chickpea snacks, and a simple beans-and-rice dinner.

pasta + noodles

Brown rice pasta and buckwheat soba noodles are quick, easy, and craveable. Toss brown rice pasta with seasonal roasted veggies, a fresh pesto, or my basic tomato sauce (page 87), and enjoy soba noodles with an Asian-style dressing or steamed vegetables, or in miso soups.

gluten-free bread + crackers

I'm not a big fan of processed food, but not all gluten-free breads and crackers are created equal. I purchase gluten-free bread from my local farmers' market and snack on flax and seed crackers often; look for ones without additives.

gluten-free flours

I keep a few gluten-free flours on hand for baking. In addition to almond meal, buckwheat and oat flours are also great. I love them for pancakes (page 82) and waffles. Chickpea flour is an excellent option for more savory uses, such as flatbreads (page 88).

dried mushrooms, seaweed + chiles

Dried mushrooms are umami powerhouses—rich in a savory flavor that adds a unique depth to broths—and they pack a nutritional punch.

Sea vegetables are anti-inflammatory and abundant in alkalinizing minerals. You will find a whole assortment in my cabinet, from kombu, arame, and hijiki to wakame and nori sheets. I add a small piece of kombu to broths, grains, and beans, which infuses them with minerals and makes them easier to digest. For the other seaweeds, I like to rehydrate and then marinate them in a little bit of gluten-free tamari and add them to vegetable bowls and salads, or stir them into miso soups.

Dried chiles are always on standby for last-minute salsas (page 36) and for adding to broths for a little kick. Beware: Know your chiles. They can vary in heat!

nutritional yeast

These bright yellow flakes are addictively cheesy and nutty and can be sprinkled all over popcorn, kale chips, pastas, and roasted veggies, and used to make vegan parmesan (page 38). This is a vegan staple—not only does it create the most delicious cheeselike flavor; it's also rich in the essential vitamin B$_{12}$, which is typically found in animal products.

oils + fats

Take a look in my cabinet and you will find all the oils I list below. I mostly cook with coconut oil, ghee, OmegaOil, and camelina oil—all of which have a high smoke point. All of the recipes in this book have the oil or fat I would recommend, but feel free to change it up to fit your taste.

I use olive oil and sesame oil mainly as finishing oils—drizzling them on vegetables or in dressings. Most oils are delicate, so take care of them by storing them in a dark, cool place.

OLIVE OIL Olive oil protects against heart disease by raising good cholesterol (HDL) and lowering bad cholesterol (LDL). Save (and splurge on!) extra-virgin olive oil for drizzling on avocado toasts, grain salads, soups, and summer vegetables.

COCONUT OIL Coconut oil is a great alternative to olive oil, and I use it frequently in cooking and baking.

It also contains lauric acid, which is a potent antibacterial that can kill not only bacteria but also viruses and fungi that have entered your body. It's a multipurpose oil that is also widely known as one of the best natural beauty products.

OMEGAOIL OmegaOil is a blended oil of olive, coconut, flax, avocado, high-oleic sunflower, and chia. It's formulated to have a high smoke point, so you can use it anywhere you currently use olive oil in cooking.

CAMELINA OIL I first discovered this wonderful, nutty oil derived from the camelina plant at the farmers' market in Portland, Oregon. It's having a comeback in part because it's packed with antioxidants and has incredibly high levels of omega-3's. It also makes an excellent cooking oil because of its high smoke point.

SESAME OIL Sesame oil is a potent antioxidant and imparts a strong nutty flavor to whatever you use it in, so I save this oil for my Asian-style dishes, dressings, soups, and stir-fries.

GHEE Ghee has been used in Ayurvedic cooking for centuries both as a cooking fat and as a health aid. To make it, you heat butter until the proteins (casein) and sugars (lactose) separate, and you are left with pure butterfat. The removal of the caseins makes ghee potentially suitable for those who have a dairy intolerance and also stabilizes it for cooking at high temperatures. Make sure you are making or purchasing ghee made from organic, grass-fed butter.

Like coconut oil, ghee is also a great beauty product—dab it under your eyes for instant moisture or rub it on mild kitchen burns in place of Neosporin.

Honey, coconut sugar, maple syrup, and dates are my favorite sweeteners to use in teas, baked goods, almond milk, and more. Keep in mind that they are still *sugar,* so it's best to use them rather sparingly or in balance with healthy fats and protein. If you are on a low- or no-sugar diet, stevia could be a good option for you.

RAW HONEY + MANUKA HONEY Raw honey and manuka honey are filled with minerals and antioxidants, and are antiviral, antibacterial, and antifungal. Pick honey up at your local farmers' market—if it is made locally, it will have special properties that may help fight local environmental allergens.

COCONUT SUGAR Coconut sugar has a lower glycemic index than regular sugar and a nice hint-of-caramel flavor. It's one of my favorite sweeteners to use in baked goods like muffins or cookies and helps create the most enviable clusters in my granola (page 180).

MAPLE SYRUP Maple syrup is a great vegan-friendly sweetener. Make candied nuts (page 39) or goji granola (page 180), or add a dash to dressings and vegetables, preroasting to enhance the flavors.

DATES Dates come in many different varieties—my favorite being medjool dates. You can find medjool dates in well-stocked markets or farmers' markets (especially in California). Look for dates that are plump and soft. Blend them into your almond milks for a hint of natural sweetness or add them to energy balls. They're also delicious whole, with a bit of almond butter stuffed in the middle.

STEVIA Stevia is a natural zero-calorie, highly concentrated sweetener that is an extract from the stevia leaf. One to two drops goes a *long* way—too much will result in a bitter or unnatural taste. Add it to your daily smoothies or elixirs.

RAW APPLE CIDER VINEGAR Raw apple cider vinegar is detoxifying and healing, and unlike other vinegars, which are acidic, raw apple cider vinegar helps your body maintain a desirable pH balance. You may notice some things floating around in the bottle, and that is *actually* good. This is known as "the mother," and it contains live enzymes. Bragg's is my brand of choice.

LOW-SODIUM GLUTEN-FREE TAMARI Tamari is a soy sauce-like seasoning that I often use in dressings and sauces. Opt for low-sodium and check the label to make sure it is gluten free (some are not). If you are avoiding soy for any reason, try out liquid coconut aminos instead.

MISO Miso is a gut-loving fermented paste that can be used in dressings, soups, and sauces. It's typically made out of fermented soy, but can also be made from non-soy sources such as brown rice and chickpeas. My favorite is the chickpea miso made by South River Miso Co. If you're purchasing a soy-based miso, go for an organic one, and always check the label—some do contain gluten.

RAW SAUERKRAUT Raw sauerkraut is made from lacto-fermented vegetables and supports gut health and digestion. I love adding it to grain bowls (page 42), salads, sandwiches, and lettuce wraps, or eating it straight out of the jar! Make your own, or head to your local farmers' market or health foods store to check out the selection.

DIJON MUSTARD Dijon mustard adds a savory kick to dressings and dips, and mustard seeds and powder are great for digestion. Look for a mustard that is free of additives.

more superfoods!

Superfoods are an easy way to add extra health benefits and nutrients to any meal. They can easily be incorporated into a variety of dishes, and you will see them used throughout many of my recipes. I recommend buying them in the bulk section of your grocery store or online, as some can be rather pricey. Don't fret if they aren't in your budget right now—all fruits and veggies are superfoods in my book!

FLAXSEEDS Flaxseeds are the greatest plant-food source of omega-3's, followed by chia seeds. They are indigestible in their whole, raw form, so you need to grind them before adding them to your dishes or soak them overnight before blending them into smoothies. Flaxseeds go rancid easily—they are relatively delicate and sensitive to light and temperature, so make sure to store them in the fridge.

CHIA SEEDS These little superseeds help keep you full and hydrated. Packed with nutrients, chia seeds are best known for providing long-lasting energy along with plenty of fiber. When soaked in water, they expand up to ten times their size. Enjoy them stirred into puddings, blended into smoothies, and sprinkled into cookies.

HEMP HEARTS Hemp hearts are an amazing source of plant protein and omega-3 fatty acids, essential for keeping the brain, skin, and heart healthy. They are anti-inflammatory and immune-boosting. They have a nutty flavor; enjoy them sprinkled on top of salads, smoothie bowls, and muffins (page 170), or straight out of the bag.

BEE POLLEN Bee pollen can be a powerful source of vitamins, minerals, antioxidants, essential amino acids, and plant proteins for those without an allergy to bees. It can soothe environmental allergies, promote skin health, nourish blood and muscles, and support fertility, stamina, and recovery. Start by blending a spoonful into smoothies or scattered on top of chia puddings. Store bee pollen in the fridge.

RAW CACAO POWDER Cacao powder is rich in minerals, mood-boosting, and supports the release of endorphins. It can be added to sweet or savory dishes—puddings, chilies, mole sauces, and more—to create depth of flavor. Read up on more benefits of this powder on page 191.

UNSWEETENED COCONUT FLAKES Coconut flakes come in two different forms—large or desiccated—and I use both frequently. They are rich in fiber, vitamins, and minerals, and can be used in both sweet and savory ways: toasted and mixed into grain salads, sprinkled on smoothie bowls, blended into milks, or in snacks and desserts like my mango macarons (page 168). Make sure to purchase unsweetened and organic coconut.

DRIED GOJI BERRIES Goji berries are packed full of antioxidants—nearly ten times more than in blueberries—making them an amazing skin-enhancing and antiaging food. Look for them dried in the bulk bins at your local natural foods store and choose berries that are slightly plump and soft. They pair perfectly with granola, chia puddings, coconut yogurt, and smoothies, or just munch on them alone.

DRIED MULBERRIES Mulberries are high in antioxidants and rich in resveratrol and vitamin C, making them cancer-fighting and antiaging. You'll find dried white mulberries at your local natural foods store, and as you would with goji berries, pick out ones that aren't completely dried out. Enjoy them alone, on top of chia puddings, or added to your favorite trail mix recipe.

CHLORELLA Chlorella is a microalgae and contains the most chlorophyll of any plant, which makes it incredibly detoxifying, blood-building, and great for digestion, skin, and the immune system. Stir it into smoothies, soups, and salad dressings, or simply drink it mixed into water in the morning.

SPICE CABINET

bay leaf —soothes digestion; add to soups and beans to deepen flavor.

chili powder —reduces inflammation and boosts immunity; add to chilies and roasted sweet potatoes.

red pepper flakes —revs metabolism, boosts immunity, and clears congestion; add a pinch to avocado toasts, pastas, and pizzas.

turmeric —boosts immunity, is antibacterial and anti-inflammatory; add a dash to smoothies and use in dressings and curries.

coriander —aids in digestion, lowers cholesterol; add to soups, curries, and falafel.

cinnamon —balances blood sugar; add to smoothies or sprinkle on top of fruit.

cumin —contains anti-inflammatory antioxidants and helps with digestion; add to soups, stews, and roasted vegetables.

cayenne —revs up your circulation, metabolism, and immune system; add a pinch to anything for heat.

cardamom —contains beneficial minerals; pair it with cacao and cinnamon for a delicious treat.

oregano —works as a potent natural antibacterial; add to chilies and stews.

pure vanilla extract —is high in antioxidants; add to plant-based milks, chia puddings, and desserts.

black pepper —supports digestion and relieves congestion, works in tandem with turmeric to help absorb all its good stuff; add to dishes to bring out the flavor.

salt —Natural salts win over your average table salt because they contain trace minerals that benefit the body. They also won't contain anticaking agents or synthetic additives that are mixed into other salts.

SEA SALT Sea salt is made from evaporated seawater. One type is Celtic salt—a grayish sea salt that has a wet feel to it since it retains a bit of water. My standby is Maldon, a flaky sea salt. It's a finishing salt, meaning you add it to dishes at the end to bring out the flavors. I love to sprinkle it on avocado toasts, and I keep a little dish of it on my counter to add another pop of flavor to salads, vegetables, and more.

PINK SALT Pink salt is rich in trace minerals and is known for its healing properties. It gets its color mainly from the presence of iron oxide, along with other trace minerals. Unlike regular table salt, pink salt works as an electrolyte, helps regulate pH, stimulates circulation, lowers blood pressure, and detoxifies the body. I keep fine pink salt on hand, as well as pink salt with a larger grain, and add pinches of one or the other to just about everything.

back to basics

these recipes are your building blocks. Not sure how to cook beans that don't come from a can? Or how the perfectly cooked brown rice was made at your favorite restaurant? This chapter has you covered.

By mastering the basics, you'll build confidence in the kitchen and unleash hundreds of healthy dishes that you can prepare in a snap. Set aside some time on Sundays to whip up a batch of beans and grains and whisk up a few dressings. You'll be more than ready for the week ahead.

Beans and lentils are good sources of plant-based protein and fiber. Opening a can is convenient, but cooking them from scratch is almost as simple, and you'll notice a difference in texture and flavor. I like to add a small piece of kombu to the pot, which can help make beans and lentils more digestible. Use the chart below as a basic guideline for cooking times.

serving varies; makes 2 to 3 cups depending on variety

ingredients

1 cup (185 g) dried beans or lentils

1 small piece kombu

Sea salt or pink salt

method

Choose your variety of bean or lentil. Sort through and discard any broken ones, stones, and debris. Rinse the beans or lentils in a strainer under running water until the water runs clear.

Put them in a heavy-bottomed pot and add enough cold water to cover them by about the length of your thumb.

Bring the water to a boil and cook for 3 minutes.

If you are cooking beans: Remove the pot from the heat and let it stand for an hour.

Drain and rinse the beans, then add them back to the pot and cover them with cold water as before. Add the kombu, bring the water to a boil, cover the pot, and simmer until the beans are nearly tender (see chart). When they still have some bite, add salt to taste and simmer uncovered for 5 minutes longer or until they're cooked through.

If you are cooking lentils: Add the kombu, reduce the heat to a simmer, and continue cooking. When the lentils are nearly cooked through (see chart), add salt to taste and cook uncovered for 5 minutes longer.

Use cooked beans and lentils in salads, vegetable bowls, and soups. Store leftovers in the fridge or freezer, with beans ideally in their cooking liquid. They will last up to 5 days in the fridge or up to 3 months in the freezer.

note:
Cooking time can vary, depending on the size and age of your bean, so make sure you test along the way, and continue to simmer until completely cooked.

DRIED BEAN + LENTIL	AVERAGE COOKING TIME
black beans	50 minutes
chickpeas	90 minutes
kidney beans	50 minutes
mung beans	50 minutes
navy beans	50 minutes
black lentils	20 minutes
french green (du puy) lentils	20 minutes
green lentils	20 minutes
red lentils	20 minutes

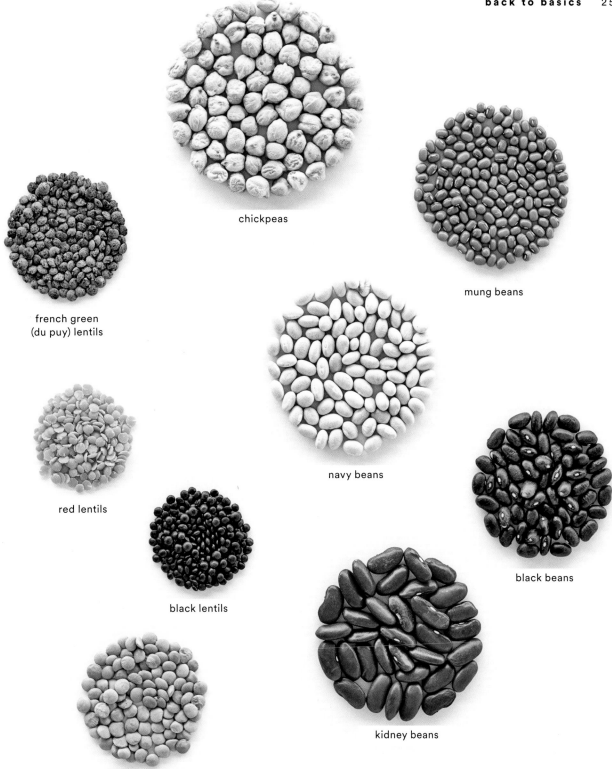

chickpeas

mung beans

french green
(du puy) lentils

navy beans

red lentils

black beans

black lentils

kidney beans

green lentils

grains

The key to making the perfect pot of grains is to leave it alone when it's cooking! If you stir it even once, your grains will end up unevenly cooked or, worse, mushy. I also recommend soaking them beforehand. Grains contain phytic acid, which binds to important minerals and prevents you from absorbing their nutrients; soaking reduces the phytic acid, and makes for more nutritious, easier-to-digest meals.

serving varies; makes 2 to 4 cups depending on grain

ingredients

1 cup (190 g) dried grain of your choice (see Note for wild rice)

Splash of apple cider vinegar or lemon juice, if soaking

½ teaspoon sea salt or pink salt

method

Choose your dried grain. Rinse the grains in a fine-mesh strainer, rubbing them together with your fingers until the water runs clear.

To soak the grain, cover it with 2 cups (480 ml) warm water and the apple cider vinegar or lemon juice (a nice splash or squeeze—no need to measure). Stir and soak for up to 24 hours. Rinse and drain the grain.

Put dry grains in a pot with 2 cups (480 ml) water or soaked grains with 1⅔ cups (405 ml) water; add the salt and bring it to a boil. Reduce the heat, cover, and let the grains simmer until they are cooked through and the water is absorbed.

Remove the pot from the heat and place a kitchen (or paper) towel between the pot and lid for 5 minutes. Fluff the grains with a fork and serve.

note:
The exception to this method is wild rice, which should be cooked with 3 cups (720 ml) water instead of 2 cups (480 ml). It can also be cooked like pasta and drained, if there is excess water.

GRAIN	AVERAGE COOKING TIME (if soaking, cooking time will be reduced by 5 to 10 minutes)
buckwheat	20 minutes
quinoa	15 minutes
wild rice	45 to 60 minutes
brown rice	30 to 50 minutes
black rice	40 to 50 minutes
millet	20 to 30 minutes
rolled oats	10 to 20 minutes
steel cut oats	20 to 30 minutes

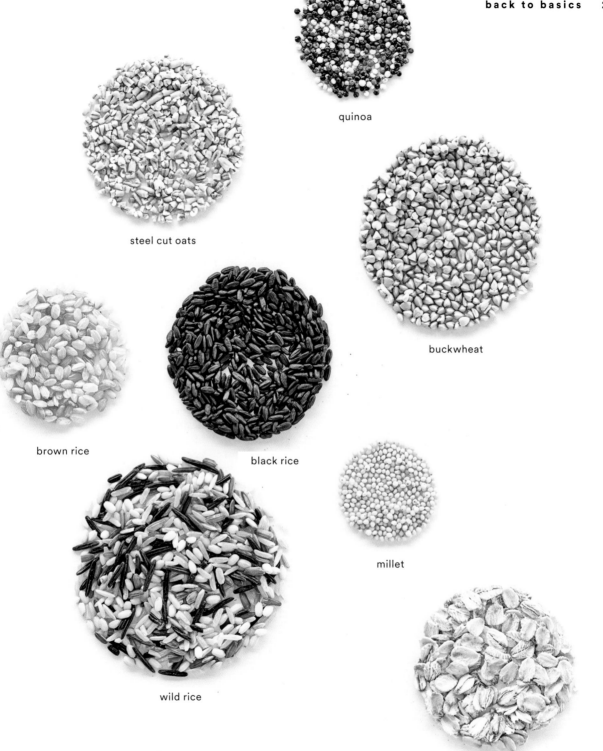

quinoa

steel cut oats

buckwheat

brown rice

black rice

millet

wild rice

rolled oats

Now that you've mastered beans and grains, it's time to move on to the art of veggies. There are endless ways to prepare veggies—here are a few of my favorites.

roasted vegetables

Roasting vegetables is one of my favorite ways to prep them—you can roast a variety of veggies on the same tray at the same time! Among the best vegetables to roast are broccoli, Brussels sprouts, carrots, cauliflower, sweet potatoes, squash . . . the list goes on. The best part about these is, like their bean and grain counterparts, they last for a few days in the fridge.

ingredients

Assorted vegetables of your choice

Oil of your choice

Sea salt or pink salt

Freshly ground black pepper

Garlic cloves and fresh herbs as desired for flavoring

method

Preheat the oven to 400°F (205°C) and line a rimmed baking sheet (or two) with parchment. (Lining the baking sheet isn't necessary but makes for easy cleanup.)

Cut all your veggies about the same size so they will cook evenly. This can be 1- to 2-inch (2.5- to 5-cm) pieces, matchsticks, or even whole if it's a small vegetable like baby carrots or Brussels sprouts. The larger your pieces, the longer they will take to cook.

Toss the veggies with oil until they are just coated and season them with salt and pepper. Feel free to add in whole cloves of garlic and herbs like thyme and rosemary for extra flavor.

Spread the vegetables evenly on the prepared baking sheet. You want them to have some room to breathe—if they are too crowded, they won't crisp up nicely, which is especially important when you are baking something like sweet potato fries.

Roast the veggies until they're cooked through. Your veggies will be done in 35 to 45 minutes, depending on the size. Give them a stir a couple of times during roasting to check on them and help them cook evenly.

steamed vegetables + greens

Steamed vegetables prove that sometimes simple is best. They cook faster than roasted veggies (no thirty-minutes-or-more wait for dinner to be ready), and they also store incredibly well for snacks and dinners later in the week. They are the perfect addition to grain bowls and salads. My favorite vegetables and greens to steam are carrots, squash, broccoli, sweet potatoes, green beans, and dark, leafy greens like kale and collards.

ingredients

Assorted vegetables of your choice

method

Cut the vegetables into relatively the same size pieces and group vegetables with similar densities together. (For example, broccoli and cauliflower.)

Fill a pot with about 1 inch (2.5 cm) water and insert your steamer basket. Make sure the water does not touch the basket. If it does, reduce the amount of water before proceeding.

Bring the water to a boil and add the first vegetables. The densest vegetables, like carrots and sweet potatoes, should go in first. Cover the pot and reduce the heat to medium-low. After a few minutes, add less-dense vegetables like broccoli and green beans. Cover and continue cooking. When these vegetables are almost cooked through, add any dark, leafy greens. These will take the shortest amount of time to steam.

Cooking time will vary depending on the size and type of your vegetables. As a rule of thumb, sweet potatoes, squash, and carrots take 8 to 10 minutes; broccoli and green beans, about 5 minutes; and dark, leafy greens, about 3 minutes.

tip:
Add a squeeze of lemon to steamed greens—the vitamin C of the lemon juice will help you absorb the iron found in your greens.

cauli-rice

makes about 4 cups (400 g)

It's pretty hard to believe that cauliflower can transform into a soft, fluffy rice, but it's true! In fact, it hardly resembles its crunchy former self and can take the place of rice in many dishes, whether it's a stir-fry, burrito bowl, tabbouleh salad, or pilaf. It takes just a few minutes and a food processor to make this happen. If you don't have a food processor, you can also chop the cauliflower by hand or grate it— the florets will break up naturally into ricelike pieces!

ingredients

1 head white, yellow, green, or purple cauliflower

1 tablespoon coconut oil or ghee

Pinch of sea salt or pink salt

Pinch of freshly ground black pepper

method

Start by cutting off the green leaves of the cauliflower, dividing it in half, and cutting it into florets. You can include some of the inner core with the florets.

Place a handful of the florets into a food processor and pulse until the cauliflower resembles rice grains. Don't overload the food processor, or else you will not get an even pulse on the cauliflower. Use a spatula to transfer the cauliflower to a bowl and repeat with the remaining florets (this usually takes two or three batches total, depending on the size of your cauliflower and food processor). You can also use a high-speed blender by blending on low and gently pressing the cauliflower into the blades with a tamper.

At this point, you can serve the cauli-rice raw, or you can cook it, which is what I prefer. Heat a large skillet over medium. Add the oil or ghee, then stir in the cauli-rice with the salt and pepper. Cook for 5 to 7 minutes, or until tender.

Alternatively, you can toss the cauli-rice in the oil, with the salt and pepper, and roast in the oven at 375°F (190°C) for 20 to 25 minutes, or until the cauli-rice starts to turn golden.

Serve immediately or store in the fridge for up to 4 days.

note:
Make sure your cauliflower is super dry before ricing. You can pat excess moisture out with a towel after you rice it before serving or cooking.

veggie noodles

serving varies; 1 medium-size vegetable serves 1

In a matter of seconds, you can watch vegetables become beautiful spirals of noodles with the help of a simple tool. Spiralizers are versatile for lots of veggies, and there are a number of models to choose from— I use the Inspiralizer—including small handheld versions. Another option would be to use a julienne peeler (which works well for zucchini, summer squash, daikon radish, cucumber, and carrots). For best results when spiralizing, use a vegetable that is nearly 2 inches (5 cm) wide and at least that long as well. You can try spiralizing other veggies, but these are the ones that I prepare most often.

ingredients

1 zucchini

1 summer squash

1 daikon radish

method

Spiralize noodles using your spiralizer of choice. Enjoy raw or follow one of the cooking suggestions in the chart below.

VEGETABLE	PREFERRED METHOD
large carrots	serve raw, roast at 375°F (190°C) for 15 minutes, or sauté for 7 to 10 minutes
cucumber	serve raw
zucchini	serve raw or sauté for 2 minutes
summer squash	serve raw or sauté for 2 minutes
daikon radish	add to soups and simmer for 3 to 5 minutes
sweet potato	roast at 375°F (190°C) for 15 to 20 minutes or sauté for 7 to 10 minutes

These recipes are basics to have in your rotation. They add flavor to the simplest dishes and are at home on salads, vegetable bowls, pastas, and more. I like to choose one or two to make on the weekend to keep in the fridge for last-minute dishes throughout the week.

cfdc vinaigrette

makes about 1 cup (240 ml)

It's important to have a signature dressing—one you keep in your back pocket and can whip up at a moment's notice. This is what is always on hand at my house for simple green salads or even to drizzle over veggies. I like it heavy on the lemon for a tangier flavor, but feel free to adjust it to your own taste.

ingredients

½ small shallot, finely minced

Juice of 2 lemons

½ cup (120 ml) olive oil

2 teaspoons Dijon mustard

Sea salt or pink salt

Freshly ground black pepper

method

Combine the shallot and lemon juice in a jar and let sit for about 10 minutes. Whisk in the olive oil and Dijon; season with salt and pepper to taste.

miso-ginger dressing

makes about 1 cup (240 ml)

This dressing transforms anything you are eating into an instantly craveable, never-want-to-stop-eating dish. It's also great on crunchy salads and slaws and drizzled on top of steamed vegetables and spiralized noodles.

ingredients

¼ cup (60 ml) sesame oil

2 tablespoons olive oil

Juice of 2 limes

¼ cup (60 ml) chickpea miso (see Note, page 142)

2 tablespoons low-sodium gluten-free tamari

1 tablespoon apple cider vinegar

2-inch (5-cm) piece fresh ginger, peeled and roughly chopped

method

In a blender, blend the dressing ingredients together until smooth, about 30 seconds. (If you do not have a blender, finely mince or grate the ginger and then whisk the ingredients together.)

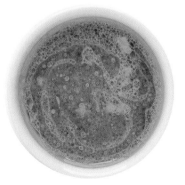

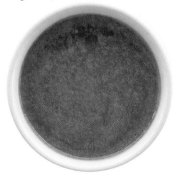

turmeric-tahini dressing

makes about 1 cup (240 ml)

There's something so fun about drizzling a beautifully bright yellow, velvety tahini dressing on veggies. Not only is it pretty; it's laced with extra immune-boosting power from turmeric. I always find myself making big batches of this dressing in the winter for steamed veggies and greens.

ingredients

¼ cup (60 ml) tahini

Juice of 2 lemons

2 tablespoons olive oil

½ teaspoon ground turmeric

Dash of cayenne

Dash of maple syrup

Sea salt or pink salt

Freshly ground black pepper

method

In a small bowl, combine the tahini, lemon juice, olive oil, turmeric, cayenne, maple syrup, and 2 tablespoons water and whisk together. Slowly drizzle in up to 2 tablespoons additional water, until the dressing reaches your desired consistency, creamy but pourable. Season with salt and pepper to taste.

cfdc hot sauce

makes about 2¼ cups (540 ml)

Skip the store-bought sriracha—the most popular kind is laden with preservatives. Instead, make a batch of this.

ingredients

1 tablespoon coconut oil

1 pound jalapeño peppers

5 garlic cloves, minced

½ cup apple cider vinegar

1 tablespoon sea salt or pink salt

2 tablespoons maple syrup

¼ to ½ cup (8 to 16 g) cilantro

method

In a large heavy-bottomed skillet or pot, heat the coconut oil over medium-high. Add the jalapeño and garlic to the pan. Sauté for 5 minutes. Transfer the mixture to a blender.

Puree the jalapeño mixture with the apple cider vinegar, ½ cup (120 ml) water, and the salt. Transfer back to the skillet, bring to a boil, and simmer for 10 minutes.

Let cool slightly before transferring back to the blender with the maple syrup and cilantro. Blend until completely smooth. Taste and adjust seasoning as desired. Store in a jar in the fridge for 2 to 3 weeks, or for a few months in the freezer.

carol's salsa roja

makes about 2 cups (480 ml)

My aunt Carol always makes the best tacos when I visit the family out in LA. But my favorite part of taco night? Her salsa, and she was happy to share her go-to recipe with me. The heat level will depend on what type of chiles you use and how many seeds you leave in.

ingredients

> 3 dried chiles (I prefer 1 ancho or pasilla chile and 2 guajillo chiles)
>
> ½ white onion, chopped
>
> 2 garlic cloves, peeled and left whole
>
> 1 tomato, roughly chopped
>
> ¼ cup (8 g) cilantro
>
> Juice of 1 lime
>
> Sea salt or pink salt

method

Remove the seeds and stems of the chiles, then soak them in hot water for 30 minutes. Add the chiles, onion, garlic, and tomato to a small saucepan and add just enough water to cover the chiles. Bring it to a boil, then simmer until the chiles are soft all the way through, about 20 minutes. Let the mixture cool slightly, then transfer it to a blender and puree until smooth. Blend in the cilantro, lime, and salt to taste. Let chill in the fridge before serving. Store in a jar in the fridge for up to 5 days.

roasted tomatillo salsa

makes about 2 cups (480 ml)

This simple salsa recipe is a game-changer. It's perfect with Mexi-Cali breakfast bowls (page 80) or sweet potato fries (page 164), on tacos, and even as an enchilada sauce.

ingredients

> 6 to 8 fresh tomatillos (about ¾ pound/340 g)
>
> 1 jalapeño
>
> 2 garlic cloves, peels left on
>
> ½ white onion, quatered and layers seperated
>
> Juice of 1 lime
>
> Sea salt or pink salt

method

Preheat the broiler and place the rack close to the top. Line a rimmed baking sheet with foil.

Remove and discard the husks from the tomatillos and rinse them under warm water. Broil the tomatillos, jalapeño, garlic, and onion on the prepared baking sheet, turning once, until the tomatillos are lightly charred, 7 to 10 minutes. Let cool slightly, then remove the stem from the jalapeño and the skins from the garlic.

Puree the broiled vegetables in a food processor or blender until smooth. Season with the lime juice and salt to taste. Let chill in the fridge before serving. Store in a jar in the fridge for up to 5 days.

cfdc pesto

makes about ¾ cup (180 ml)

Pesto adds a punch of flavor to any dish. Try out different nuts and greens in the same ratio, depending on the season (toasted pepitas and kale in the fall or pistachios and arugula in the summer).

ingredients

1 head garlic

¼ cup (35 g) pine nuts

1 cup (40 g) packed basil

¼ cup (60 ml) extra-virgin olive oil

Juice of ½ lemon, more as needed

Sea salt or pink salt

2 tablespoons vegan parm (optional, page 38)

Pinch of red pepper flakes (optional)

method

To roast the garlic, preheat the oven to 375°F (190°C). Peel away the papery skin, and trim the garlic head to reveal the tops of the cloves. Wrap it in foil, and bake for 45 to 60 minutes, or until they are soft and almost caramelized. Let cool and remove the cloves by pressing at the bottom.

Put 5 cloves into a food processor, reserving the rest for another use, and add the pine nuts, basil, oil, lemon juice, ½ teaspoon salt, the vegan parm, and red pepper flakes (if you're using them). Taste and add more salt, lemon, or olive oil as needed. Store in the fridge for up to a week or in the freezer for up to 6 months.

In addition to the dressing, the "crunch" is perhaps what makes a dish so satisfying. Layering textures in food can be as simple as adding just one of these crunchy items. Keep them on hand to add a kick to any meal.

vegan parm

makes about 1 cup (150 g)

Parmesan cheese has an umami quality that completely transforms any dish it hits. Your perfect bowl of pasta just wouldn't be the same without it. Use this parm wherever you would normally use the real deal, and you won't even think twice.

ingredients

¾ cup (90 g) cashews

¼ cup (40 g) hemp hearts

¼ cup (15 g) nutritional yeast

1 teaspoon sea salt or pink salt

½ teaspoon garlic powder

method

Combine all ingredients in a food processor or high-speed blender and pulse until the mixture turns into a crumbly, fine meal, about 15 seconds. Store in an airtight container in the fridge, and it will last for a few weeks.

gomasio

makes about 1 cup (130 g)

Sesame seeds are an amazing source of calcium, iron, and protein. Sprinkle this macrobiotic staple on just about anything (like whole grains and vegetables) for a delicious nutrition boost.

ingredients

1 cup (125 g) brown and black sesame seeds (I like using half of each)

2 teaspoons fine sea salt or pink salt

method

Place the sesame seeds in a heavy-bottomed or cast-iron skillet over medium heat.

Cook for 7 to 10 minutes, stirring constantly, until you see the brown seeds start to turn golden brown. They will also start popping around the pan, which is a good indicator they are toasted. Pour the seeds onto a plate and allow them to cool to room temperature.

Place the seeds and salt in a food processor and pulse, or grind them in mortar and pestle, until the mixture has a coarse texture.

Transfer the gomasio to a glass container and store in the fridge for 1 to 2 months.

tamari almonds

makes 2 cups (280 g)

This savory snack is perfect eaten alone or used as a topping on your veggie bowls, Asian-style noodles, and more!

ingredients

> 2 cups (280 g) raw almonds, soaked overnight in water
>
> 2 tablespoons low-sodium gluten-free tamari
>
> ½ teaspoon coconut sugar
>
> Dash of cayenne
>
> Dash of ground turmeric

method

Preheat the oven to 300°F (150°C). Line a baking sheet with parchment and evenly spread the almonds onto it. Bake them for 10 minutes.

Meanwhile, combine the tamari, coconut sugar, cayenne, and turmeric in a mixing bowl and set aside. Remove the almonds from the oven and immediately toss them in the mixing bowl with the tamari mixture. Pop them back into the oven and bake them for another 15 minutes, or until the almonds are dry and cooked through (when you bite into one, it should be slightly golden throughout).

Let the almonds cool completely before storing them in an airtight container. They will stay fresh for a few weeks.

candied walnuts

makes 1 cup (110 g)

Add a touch of sweetness to your morning breakfast porridges and oatmeals. You can also crumble the walnuts on top of smoothie bowls and ice cream, or toss them into kale salads and veggie bowls.

ingredients

> 1 cup (100 g) walnuts
>
> 2 tablespoons maple syrup
>
> Sea salt or pink salt

method

Heat a heavy-bottomed pan to medium. Add the walnuts and toast, stirring constantly for 3 to 4 minutes. Add the maple syrup and a pinch or two of salt. Stir constantly until the maple syrup starts to thicken and caramelize, 2 to 3 minutes; be very careful not to burn the walnuts!

Spread them out on parchment paper and let them cool. Store in an airtight container for up to 2 weeks.

smashed cucumbers

This salad is a fresh complement to noodles and rice bowls, but it's also satisfying on its own as an afternoon snack or as a BBQ side dish. It's easy to multiply for a crowd.

ingredients

7 Persian cucumbers (about 16 ounces/500 g)

Sea salt or pink salt

1 tablespoon sesame oil

1 tablespoon apple cider vinegar

½ teaspoon honey

½ teaspoon chickpea miso

½ teaspoon brown sesame seeds

½ teaspoon black sesame seeds

Pinch of red pepper flakes

Handful of torn mint, plus more for serving

method

Trim the ends off the cucumbers, cut them in half lengthwise, then cut them into 1-inch (2.5-cm) pieces. Smash each piece with the side of a wide knife blade (make sure the sharp edge is facing away from you). Transfer the cucumbers to a bowl and stir in ½ teaspoon salt. Let them sit for 20 minutes before draining off the liquid. Set aside.

Whisk together the sesame oil, vinegar, honey, and miso in a small bowl. Pour the mixture over the cucumbers. Add the sesame seeds, red pepper flakes, and mint, and stir well. Taste and adjust the seasoning, adding a pinch more salt as needed. Chill for at least 15 minutes and garnish with additional fresh mint before serving.

simple slaw

serves about 4

I hesitate to call this a recipe—it's so simple! But I've included it here because I make it all the time (and it's great for using up extra red cabbage). This slaw is the easiest way to add crunch to your tacos, salads, and burrito bowls. You can add other crunchy veggies like carrots and radishes to the mix or herbs like cilantro before serving—just adjust the seasoning accordingly.

ingredients

½ head red cabbage, thinly shredded

Juice of 1 to 2 limes

Sea salt or pink salt

method

Combine the cabbage and lime juice in a bowl. Mix well and season with a pinch or two of salt. Store in the fridge for up to 3 days.

quick-pickled radishes

makes enough to fill a ½-pint (250-ml) jar

These radishes will add a tangy, addictive crunch to any dish. You can use a mandoline to slice the radishes—watch your fingers!—or simply use a sharp knife. I love them on top of tacos, bowls, salads, and more.

ingredients

½ cup (120 ml) apple cider vinegar

2 tablespoons maple syrup

2 teaspoons sea salt or pink salt

1 bunch radishes, trimmed and thinly sliced

method

Combine the vinegar, maple syrup, salt, and 1 cup (240 ml) water in a small saucepan over medium heat and stir. Bring to a boil, then reduce the heat and simmer for 1 minute.

Add the radishes to a medium-size jar and pour the vinegar mixture over the radishes. Allow them to cool to room temperature, about an hour. Cover the jar with the lid and refrigerate. They will keep in the fridge for a few weeks.

build your own bowl!

Spend just a little time prepping some of these ingredients in advance, and you'll be able to whip up endless combinations in no time. It's hard to go wrong here if you follow this simple formula: Choose a base, a protein, some greens, some toppings, extras, and a dressing.

BASE

brown rice

quinoa

wild rice

cauli-rice
(page 31)

PROTEIN / LEGUME

pan-fried tofu
(page 95)

poached egg
(page 81)

roasted
chickpeas
(page 123)

white beans

lentils
(page 24 or 156)

GREENS

romaine

kale

spinach

arugula

snap peas

steamed
green beans

steamed
broccoli

basil

cilantro

TOPPINGS

cherry
tomatoes

zucchini
ribbons

julienned
carrots

julienned
cucumber

julienned
pepper

roasted
golden beets

roasted
brussels
sprouts

roasted
delicata squash

avocado

roasted
butternut
squash

EXTRAS

gomasio
(page 38)

vegan parm
(page 38)

tamari almonds
(page 39)

candied
walnuts
(page 39)

simple slaw
(page 41)

pickled
radishes
(page 41)

sunflower
sprouts

microgreens

DRESSINGS

miso-ginger
dressing
(page 34)

cfdc vinaigrette
(page 34)

turmeric-tahini
dressing
(page 35)

cfdc pesto
(page 37)

cfdc hot sauce
(page 35)

spring bowl

brown rice,
pan-fried tofu,
raw veggies
(carrots, cucumber, snap peas, red pepper),
avocado,
cilantro,
sunflower sprouts,
miso-ginger dressing

summer bowl

quinoa,
cherry tomatoes,
zucchini ribbons,
arugula,
steamed green beans,
poached egg,
vegan parm,
cfdc pesto

fall bowl

wild rice,
spinach,
roasted chickpeas,
roasted butternut squash,
roasted Brussels sprouts,
tamari almonds,
turmeric-tahini dressing

winter bowl

cauli-rice,
lentils,
kale,
roasted golden beets,
candied walnuts,
pickled radishes,
cfdc vinaigrette

plant-based milks

I love making my own milks at home. It takes only a few simple steps (and tools), and the payoff is well worth it. The milk is so creamy and delicious. The best part of making nut milk is that you can play endlessly with flavor combinations that you won't find anywhere in a store. Once you master the basic ratios, let loose and experiment. Since homemade nut milk doesn't use preservatives, it won't last as long in the fridge as store-bought milk. You can add a little coconut oil to each batch, which will act as a natural antifungal, antibacterial, and preservative, prolonging its life for up to a week.

makes 3 to 4 cups (720 to 960 ml)

ingredients

basic nut milk:

1 cup (140 g) raw almonds, brazil nuts, cashews, hazelnuts, or pepitas

Sea salt or pink salt

1 teaspoon coconut oil (optional preservative)

for vanilla almond milk:

1 cup (140 g) raw almonds

2 to 3 pitted medjool dates (omit for unsweetened)

1 teaspoon pure vanilla extract

Dash of ground cinnamon

Pinch of sea salt or pink salt

for hazelnut hemp milk:

½ cup (70 g) raw hazelnuts

½ cup (75 g) hemp hearts

2 to 3 pitted medjool dates

for coconut cashew milk:

½ cup (60 g) raw cashews

½ cup (45 g) unsweetened coconut flakes

2 to 3 pitted medjool dates

Dash of cardamom

Pinch of sea salt or pink salt

pepitas

soaked almonds

raw almonds

raw cashews

coconut flakes

method

Place the nuts or seeds for your chosen milk in a jar and fill it with filtered water to cover, along with a couple pinches of salt. Let the mixture soak overnight or for at least 8 hours. Drain, rinse, and add the nuts to the blender with 3 cups (720 ml) of filtered water. Add any additional ingredients called for if you're making one of the flavored milks. Blend for 1 minute on high.

Line a medium bowl with a nut milk bag and strain the blended milk. Gently squeeze and twist the bag until it has released all of the milk (see Notes). Thin the milk with additional filtered water as desired (see Notes).

Store nut milk in a glass jar or bottle in the fridge for 2 to 3 days. If you've added the coconut oil, it will last a few more days. Shake well before enjoying.

notes:

There are a few exceptions to this method. For coconut milk, you can follow the same directions for basic nut milk, but you may enjoy a higher ratio of unsweetened coconut flakes (up to 2 cups/180 g) to water. If you are making milk with only cashews, it's not necessary to strain after blending.

You can control how creamy your milk is by adjusting the amount of filtered water you add. I like it creamier for lattes and less creamy for smoothies (with more water added, it lasts for more smoothies!).

If you want to reserve the nut pulp for another use and don't want it to be flavored or sweetened, you can blend the soaked nuts and water, strain and set aside the pulp, then reblend the milk with the flavorings. Nut pulp will last a few days in the fridge. Use it as is in smoothies or stirred into oatmeal, or even as a gentle face scrub.

tip:

If you don't have any medjool dates on hand, you can sweeten milks to taste with raw honey or maple syrup.

Homemade broths elevate soups and grains to a new level. I like to make a couple of big batches of broth and store them in quart-size containers in the freezer for easy use. If you do opt to use store-bought when you're in a pinch, choose low-sodium varieties and read the labels to avoid added sugars. Here are three of my go-to broths, which can be sipped alone or used in many of the recipes in this book.

basic veggie broth

makes 2 quarts (2 L)

This simple, clean broth is perfect for your classic vegetable soups and to cook grains in. It's versatile and easy to make in large batches.

ingredients

1 tablespoon coconut oil or ghee

2 onions, coarsely chopped

3 carrots, coarsely chopped

3 stalks celery, coarsely chopped

2 sprigs of fresh thyme

1 bay leaf

method

Heat a large pot over medium. Add the oil and sauté the onions, carrots, and celery until they're soft, about 10 minutes. Add the thyme, bay leaf, and 2 quarts (2 L) water and simmer for an hour. Strain and let cool before covering and storing it. The broth can be kept in the fridge for 5 days or frozen for 4 months.

note:
The less water you use the more flavorful the broth. The more water, the lighter the broth. I also like to leave my broth unsalted and season before using. This recipe can easily be doubled and frozen.

vegan bone broth

makes 2 quarts (2 L)

My vegan "bone broth" obviously does not contain bones, but it does make a mineral-rich, nourishing broth. This is thanks to the addition of wakame seaweed, one of the most mineral-dense foods. Turmeric and ginger create a warming broth to help fight inflammation and boost immunity.

ingredients

1 tablespoon coconut oil

2 stalks celery, chopped

1 large leek, chopped

2 garlic cloves, smashed

½-inch (12-mm) piece fresh turmeric, thinly sliced

½-inch (12-mm) piece fresh ginger, thinly sliced

1 golden beet, chopped

1 bay leaf

A few sprigs of thyme

1 tablespoon dried wakame, reconstituted in a little water

method

Heat the oil in a large stockpot over medium. Add the celery, leek, garlic, turmeric, and ginger, and sauté for 5 minutes. Add the beet, bay leaf, thyme, and 2 quarts (2 L) water. Add the wakame to the pot. Bring to a near boil, then reduce the heat to low and let the broth simmer for an hour or two (increased time will deepen the flavor). Strain the broth into another pot and let it cool before covering and storing it. The broth can be kept in the fridge for 5 days or frozen for 4 months.

tip:
I love to keep a huge pot of this broth in the fridge, sipping on it and making quick miso soups throughout the week. I leave it unseasoned, and just add some miso paste or a sprinkle of pink salt before serving.

dashi

makes 2 quarts (2 L)

Dashi is a great base for miso soup and other earthy soups and stews. My pantry is always stocked with kombu and shiitake mushrooms so I can whip this up at a moment's notice.

ingredients

1 leek, cleaned and thinly sliced

4-inch (10-cm) piece kombu

5 dried shiitake mushrooms

method

In a large pot over medium-high heat, add the leek, kombu, and mushrooms and cover with 2 quarts (2 L) cold filtered water. Bring the water to a boil, then reduce the heat to low and simmer for 45 minutes. Let the dashi cool slightly before straining it into another pot. Allow it to cool fully before covering and storing it. The broth can be kept in the fridge for 5 days or frozen for 4 months.

awaken

do you ever have superhuman days with boundless amounts of energy? Days when you feel like you can check anything and everything off your to-do list, run all of your errands, and still have energy to work out at the end of the day? These are often balanced out by slower, sluggish days when you want to stay in bed all morning and end up staring at a computer screen most of the afternoon in a not-so-productive trance.

Luckily, I have a few tricks up my sleeve that I turn to now. They've helped me get into the groove of more and more of those boundless-energy type of days. Here you'll find lots of protein-rich food and those that are high in healthy fats like beans, lentils, nuts, and chia seeds, as well as the morning rituals that get me going in the A.M. What you won't find are high doses of caffeine or coffee (except for in a body scrub!), which can end up leaving you worse for the wear.

Turn to this chapter when you could use a boost of energy or even just to maintain it throughout the day. You'll notice a difference almost immediately. For best results, eat these types of foods every day!

Props to everyone out there who is a morning person; I'm not naturally one of you. Most days I have to motivate myself to get moving (quickly!), and I've developed a routine that actually makes me feel bright-eyed and energized by the end of it. Try my go-to rituals, and if you have an extra minute, add dry brushing (page 75) to your mornings. It awakens your lymph system and increases circulation.

oil pulling

Oil pulling is an ancient Ayurvedic method that involves swishing oil around in your mouth for 15 to 20 minutes, which at first sounds like an eternity. If you're new to this, start with 2 minutes, and you'll get the hang of it in no time. Oil pulling gives your mouth a super-clean feeling and is said to improve oral hygiene as well as remove toxins and bacteria in your mouth. You may notice whiter and less sensitive teeth, more energy, and even better skin.

ingredients

> 1 tablespoon coconut oil
>
> 1 drop peppermint essential oil (optional)

method

Scoop the coconut oil onto a spoon, add the peppermint oil, then swish the mixture around in your mouth for about 20 minutes. Spit into a trash can. Rinse your mouth and brush your teeth.

lemon water

Lemons are one of nature's amazingly nutrient-dense foods and can help jump-start your digestive system in the morning. They're rich in vitamin C, boost your immune system, flush toxins from your body, and improve your skin. Lemon and warm water alone do the trick, but I like to add a splash of apple cider vinegar or ginger juice if I am feeling under the weather.

ingredients

> Juice of ½ lemon
>
> 4 to 6 ounces (120 to 180 ml) very warm water
>
> Optional add-ins:
>
> ¼ teaspoon raw honey
>
> Splash raw apple cider vinegar
>
> Fresh-pressed ginger juice
>
> Pinch of cayenne
>
> Pinch of ground turmeric

method

Combine the lemon and water in a mug and stir in any optional add-ins.

tip:

Brush your teeth before drinking your lemon water. The acid from the lemon can weaken enamel and brushing right after can remove the enamel. So brush before, and better yet, sip your drink through a glass straw.

super berry smoothie

makes 1 smoothie

My mornings are filled with personal rituals—and smoothies are often a part of them. But not all smoothies are created equal! There has to be an ideal ratio of healthy fats and protein so you aren't reaching for a snack an hour later during your 10:00 A.M. meeting. The key here is picking a clean protein powder that works for you.

ingredients

1 cup (240 ml) vanilla almond milk (page 48)

½ cup (80 g) frozen blueberries

¼ cup (65 g) frozen cherries

1 tablespoon coconut butter or almond butter

½ tablespoon maca root powder

½ tablespoon raw cacao powder

1 serving of your favorite protein powder

Dash of ground cinnamon

2 dates or raw honey to taste (optional)

method

Pour the almond milk into a blender, then add the remaining ingredients and puree until smooth.

MACA *magic*

Maca powder is made from a Peruvian root similar in appearance to a radish. This adaptogen has a uniquely nutty, caramel flavor and is rich in vitamins, minerals, and protein. It's known for increasing energy levels and mental stamina, balancing hormones, enhancing libido, and elevating mood. What's amazing about maca, and adaptogens in general, is that if you're feeling tired, it will help boost energy, but if you are feeling stressed or amped up, it can help nourish your endocrine system and bring you back to balance.

Start by adding a small amount of maca to your daily smoothie routine to help increase energy. Pair it with caramel-y flavors like nuts, dates, and cacao. One of my favorite maca smoothies (besides this one!) is frozen banana blended with almond milk, almond butter, maca, and cacao powder.

morning matcha
smoothie bowl

serves 2

Matcha is a finely ground powder of green tea known for its high level of antioxidants and its ability to provide calm, focused, and prolonged energy. The bright green powder is also rich in amino acids, an important one being L-theanine, which supports the activity of alpha brain waves. Combined with a small amount of caffeine, it leaves you feeling alert, but still cool, calm, and collected. Here, matcha powder meets its perfect match with tropical vibes of mango and coconut. Avocado might sound strange at first, but it gives the smoothie the creamiest texture.

ingredients

1 cup (240 ml) unsweetened coconut or almond milk (page 48), plus more if needed

4 handfuls spinach

2 teaspoons culinary-grade matcha powder

1 cup (165 g) frozen mango

1 banana, cut into chunks and frozen

½ avocado

Top with: cubed fresh mango, sliced kiwi, unsweetened coconut flakes, bee pollen (optional)

method

In a blender, blend the milk, spinach, and matcha until smooth. Add the mango, banana, and avocado and blend again. Add more milk to blend if needed.

Pour the smoothie into bowls and top with the fruit, coconut flakes, and, if you like, bee pollen.

chia pudding three ways—summer, fall + strawberry

serves 2

Chia pudding is a staple in my fridge. It's easy to assemble and makes the best grab-and-go breakfast or snack. My favorite base is this classic vanilla, topped with whatever fruit is in season. I also like to blend seasonal fruit or cacao powder into the base before stirring in the chia seeds, just as I've done in the strawberry version. Make it your own by assembling your chia bowl or jar as you would at an ice cream sundae bar. (Only this time with good-for-you superfoods!)

summer chia pudding

summer chia pudding

ingredients

3 tablespoons chia seeds

1 cup (240 ml) vanilla almond milk (page 48)

Raw honey

Top with: a summer berry salad of sliced peaches or nectarines, blueberries, raspberries, and few pieces of torn mint

method

Combine the chia seeds, almond milk, and honey to taste in a glass container or jar. Stir well until the chia seeds are mixed in. Place in the fridge and let sit for at least 3 hours or up to overnight. The chia seeds will expand as they soak.

In the morning, give the pudding a good stir. Top it with the fruit and a sprinkling of torn mint.

fall chia pudding

ingredients

3 tablespoons chia seeds

1 cup (240 ml) vanilla almond milk (page 48)

Raw honey

Top with: a fruit salad of cubed pear, pomegranate seeds, dried mulberries, and pepitas

method

Combine the chia seeds, almond milk, and honey to taste in a glass container or jar. Stir well until the chia seeds are mixed in. Place in the fridge and let sit for at least 3 hours or up to overnight. The chia seeds will expand as they soak.

In the morning, give the pudding a good stir. Top it with the fruit salad.

strawberry chia pudding

ingredients

1 cup (145 g) fresh or frozen strawberries

1 cup (240 ml) vanilla almond milk (page 48)

Raw honey

3 tablespoons chia seeds

Top with: sliced fresh strawberries, raw almond butter, and cacao nibs

method

In a blender, blend the strawberries, almond milk, and raw honey to taste until smooth. Strain the mixture through a fine mesh sieve or nut milk bag. Pour into a glass jar and stir in the chia seeds. Place in the fridge and let sit for at least 3 hours or up to overnight.

In the morning, give the pudding a good stir. Top it with additional strawberries, raw almond butter, and cacao nibs.

---

crazy for **CHIA**

Chia seeds are tiny powerhouses. They can expand to hold about ten times their weight in liquid, which helps you stay energized and full longer. They also aid in improving endurance and boosting your energy levels throughout the day, from staying alert during your morning meeting to showing up at your evening workout class. Chia seeds are packed with omega-3 fatty acids, fiber, and protein, and contain all nine essential amino acids, making them a "complete" protein, which is rare for a plant-based source of protein.

Pick up chia seeds at your local health foods store and look for ones that are black or white in color (but not brown, which signifies that something could be off). What's amazing about chia seeds is that when they're mixed with liquid, they turn gelatinous, making the perfect texture for breakfast puddings like the recipes above, jams and jellies, and desserts like my Mexican chocolate pudding (page 184).

fall chia pudding

strawberry chia pudding

taco salad

serves 2, with leftover taco crumble

For me, tacos are their own food group. The problem is that they don't exactly travel well during the weekday commute, which is where this taco salad comes in. It's the perfect lunch. Lentils give you energy that will last all day, thanks to their fiber content, complex carbs, and iron. Combined with the walnuts, the midday omega-3 and protein boost will have you sailing through your afternoon.

ingredients

lime dressing

2 tablespoons olive oil

Juice of 1 lime

1 teaspoon raw honey

1 garlic clove, peeled

Sea salt or pink salt

Freshly ground black pepper

walnut taco crumble

1 cup (155 g) cooked French green lentils

1 cup (100 g) walnuts

1 tablespoon low-sodium gluten-free tamari

1 teaspoon ground cumin

½ teaspoon paprika

1 tablespoon olive oil

salad

2 handfuls spinach and other mixed greens

1 small cucumber, thinly sliced

1 carrot, shredded

Handful of cherry tomatoes, halved

1 avocado, halved and thinly sliced

2 scallions, thinly sliced

Cilantro, for garnish

method

For the dressing: In a small bowl, combine the olive oil, lime juice, and honey. Smash the garlic clove and let it marinate in the mixture for 10 to 15 minutes, while you prepare the rest of the salad. Remove the garlic clove just before serving and add salt and pepper to taste.

For the walnut taco crumble: In a food processor, pulse all the ingredients until the mixture is just combined, and the texture is a rough crumble. Taste and adjust seasoning, as needed.

For the salad: Toss the greens, cucumber, carrot, and tomatoes with just enough of the lime dressing to coat the veggies. Divide the salad into two bowls and serve it with a big scoop of the walnut taco crumble, sliced avocado, scallions, and cilantro. Drizzle on the remaining dressing as desired.

WALNUTS *on the brain*

Walnuts are top dog (or nut, rather) when it comes to brain food! They are a rich source of omega-3 essential fatty acids, which is key to keeping both the brain and the heart functioning optimally. Omega-3's help us stay healthy, and since we can't produce them ourselves, we must get them from our food—like walnuts, chia seeds, flaxseeds, and hemp hearts. A lack of omega-3's in the diet can lead to inflammation, difficulty concentrating, mood disorders like depression and anxiety, and skin problems like acne.

Most of us aren't getting nearly enough omega-3's! The good news is that just a handful of walnuts serves up all that you need in a day. Walnuts are a great snack on their own; blended into smoothies; as a candied topping for chia puddings, oatmeal, and veggie bowls (page 42); or made into my walnut orange globes (page 72). They can have a bitter lining, so you may want to soak or dry-roast them before digging in.

power bowl

serves 2

I developed this bowl after a long weekend away that was filled with indulgent meals and my favorite: mezcal cocktails. My body was screaming to be brought back to a state of balance. We've all been there, and we usually find ourselves scarfing the nearest carb or breakfast sandwich to cope. As a quick—and healthier— fix, turn to a combo of protein, healthy fats, and greens. I'm not talking about a measly salad or a handful of nuts. You need an extra-satisfying bowl that's bursting with flavor and packed with everything you need to spring your body into recovery mode.

ingredients

cashew hemp dressing

½ cup (60 g) raw cashews

½ cup (75 g) hemp hearts

½ shallot, minced

1 to 2 garlic cloves

3 tablespoons olive oil

Juice of 1 lemon

½ cup (15 g) cilantro

Sea salt or pink salt

Freshly ground black pepper

salad

1 bunch curly or Tuscan kale, thinly chopped

1 tablespoon olive oil

Pinch of salt

1 carrot, finely chopped

1 Persian cucumber, diced

10 cherry tomatoes, quartered

5 oil-cured olives, pitted and roughly chopped

½ avocado, diced

serve with

1 cup (185 g) cooked quinoa, room temperature

1 cup (200 g) cooked white beans or lentils, room temperature

½ cup (50 g) simple slaw (page 41)

method

For the dressing: Soak the cashews overnight in water. Rinse, drain, and combine them with the hemp, shallot, garlic, oil, lemon juice, and cilantro in a blender. Puree the dressing, adding water to thin it to your desired consistency. Season with salt and pepper to taste. Set aside.

For the salad: To a medium bowl, add the kale, olive oil, and salt. Use your hands to massage the kale for a minute, or until it has relaxed to about half its original volume.

Add the carrot, cucumber, tomatoes, olives, and avocado to the massaged kale with about ¼ cup (60 ml) of the dressing. Gently toss the salad with your hands until it is well combined, adding additional dressing as desired.

Serve the salad topped with the quinoa, beans or lentils, and slaw.

tip:
The creamy dressing is filled with healthy fats and kicks this salad up a notch. It also doubles as a great dip if you add less water.

walnut orange globes

These little wonders are filled with brain-boosting fats and bright citrus. Citrus not only creates the most amazing flavor; *the smell* even energizes and encourages concentration. Combined with walnuts and hemp hearts, these will fuel you up for an extra-productive afternoon. Double the batch and store them in the fridge or freezer to pair with a big mug of tea when you're starting to drag—you'll want to have plenty on hand.

ingredients

½ cup (50 g) raw walnuts

½ cup (70 g) raw almonds

¾ tablespoon raw honey or maple syrup

¼ teaspoon Valencia orange zest

1 tablespoon fresh Valencia orange juice

¼ teaspoon lemon zest

Pinch of fine sea salt or pink salt

Almond milk or water, if needed

2 tablespoons hemp hearts, for rolling

method

Pulse the walnuts and almonds in a food processor until it becomes a crumbly mixture of small chunks. Add the honey, orange zest and juice, lemon zest, and salt, and blend. The mixture should stick together when pinched between your fingers. Add a splash of almond milk or water if needed.

Pour the hemp hearts into a shallow plate. Using a small cookie scoop or teaspoon, scoop the nut mixture and form it into balls, then roll each ball in the hemp hearts. Place the balls on a parchment-lined plate and chill them for 30 minutes before serving. Store them in an airtight container in the fridge for up to a week or in the freezer for 3 months.

cinnamon

coconut coffee
body scrub

coconut sugar

coconut oil

raw cacao powder

coffee grounds

coconut coffee body scrub

makes enough to fill a ½-pint (250-ml) jar

This body scrub has a permanent spot in my shower. Its exfoliating power gets rid of dead skin, and it is intensely moisturizing, leaving skin silky smooth. Like dry brushing, this scrub jump-starts your lymphatic system. By moving the lymph and improving circulation, you firm your skin and decrease the appearance of cellulite without having to move a muscle (but of course that helps too).

COFFEE GROUNDS are exfoliating and contain caffeine, which improves circulation and can help reduce the appearance of cellulite.

COCONUT SUGAR is exfoliating and helps give your skin a radiant glow.

RAW CACAO POWDER is rich in antioxidants, contains caffeine, and, teamed with coffee, helps to further improve circulation.

CINNAMON stimulates the skin and improves circulation, further reducing the appearance of cellulite.

COCONUT OIL is moisturizing and contains antibacterial and antifungal lauric acid.

ingredients

½ cup (40 g) coffee grounds

½ cup (95 g) coconut sugar

2 tablespoons raw cacao powder

½ tablespoon ground cinnamon

½ cup (120 ml) unrefined coconut oil

method

Mix all the ingredients together and store them in an airtight jar at room temperature.

To use, massage a couple of tablespoons onto wet skin, focusing on areas that are prone to cellulite (butt, thighs, etc.). Leave the scrub on for 5 to 10 minutes to intensify the effect. Rinse well.

beauty bonus:

For an extra boost to your lymphatic system, try dry brushing before hopping into the shower. Glide dry brushes over skin, working in gentle, upward motions, beginning at the feet and moving toward the heart. Brush in a clockwise motion on your stomach and a downward motion on your chest and back toward your heart.

nourish

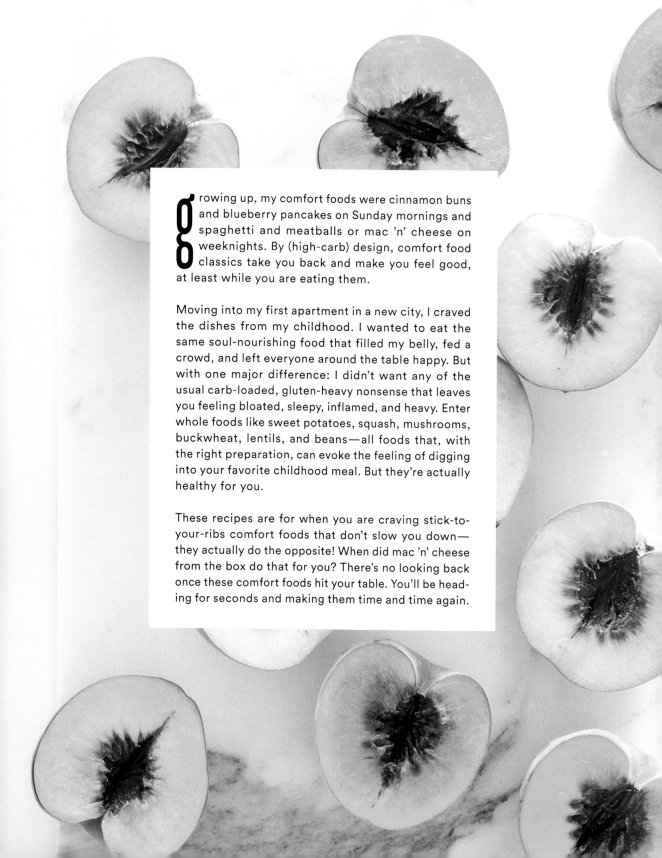

growing up, my comfort foods were cinnamon buns and blueberry pancakes on Sunday mornings and spaghetti and meatballs or mac 'n' cheese on weeknights. By (high-carb) design, comfort food classics take you back and make you feel good, at least while you are eating them.

Moving into my first apartment in a new city, I craved the dishes from my childhood. I wanted to eat the same soul-nourishing food that filled my belly, fed a crowd, and left everyone around the table happy. But with one major difference: I didn't want any of the usual carb-loaded, gluten-heavy nonsense that leaves you feeling bloated, sleepy, inflamed, and heavy. Enter whole foods like sweet potatoes, squash, mushrooms, buckwheat, lentils, and beans—all foods that, with the right preparation, can evoke the feeling of digging into your favorite childhood meal. But they're actually healthy for you.

These recipes are for when you are craving stick-to-your-ribs comfort foods that don't slow you down—they actually do the opposite! When did mac 'n' cheese from the box do that for you? There's no looking back once these comfort foods hit your table. You'll be heading for seconds and making them time and time again.

sweet as pie smoothie bowl

serves 2

This bowl is for all the pumpkin pie lovers out there. It tastes exactly like a slightly frozen, creamy version of your favorite holiday pie's filling. I love how the bright flesh of sweet potatoes creates a beautiful natural orange hue. This dish makes for a satisfying breakfast but also for an equally decadent dessert when served in small ramekins.

ingredients

¾ cup (180 ml) unsweetened almond milk (page 48), plus more if needed

1 small sweet potato, peeled, cut into chunks, steamed, and cooled

1 banana, cut into chunks and frozen

1 tablespoon raw almond butter

½ teaspoon grated, peeled fresh ginger

¼ teaspoon ground cinnamon

Few cubes of ice

Top with: additional raw almond butter, pepitas, and coconut flakes

method

Combine the milk, sweet potato, banana, almond butter, ginger, and cinnamon in a blender and puree until smooth. Adjust the milk quantity to your preferred consistency, and add a few ice cubes as desired.

Pour the smoothie into bowls and sprinkle on some or all of the toppings.

spotlight on **SWEET POTATOES**

When you think of sweet potatoes, think disease-fighting, skin-brightening, immune-boosting powerhouses. Naturally vivid orange foods (definitely not cheese puffs) signify that we're in the presence of beta-carotene, a free-radical-fighting antioxidant that is converted to vitamin A when it enters the bloodstream. Vitamin A helps strengthen the immune system, protect the eyes, and support healthy skin. Sweet potatoes are also filled with fiber and slow-release carbs that help keep you full longer.

Roast and serve them for an easy dinner, steam them (as in this recipe), or make one of my all-time favs—fries (page 164). Add some ghee (or coconut oil) when you're cooking these or before serving—a little healthy fat will help keep your blood sugar stable and help you absorb all the good stuff from the sweet potatoes.

mexi-cali breakfast bowls

serves 2

Huevos rancheros will forever be my first choice on any brunch menu. It is by no means the worst thing you can order, but it tends to be greasy and fried. This bowl is a good alternative. Both the hash and the vegan crema can be made the night before—and easily doubled or tripled for a crowd, so when your friends roll up in the morning hungry for brunch, all you have to do is poach the eggs. For my vegan friends: Sub half an avocado sprinkled with flaky sea salt and fresh lime juice for the poached egg. It will add the creamy, rich note that makes the bowl next-level.

ingredients

sweet potato hash

1 sweet potato, skin
on if organic, cut into
½-inch (12-mm) cubes

2 tablespoons coconut
oil or ghee, melted

1 teaspoon chili powder

Sea salt or pink salt

1 red onion, diced

2 garlic cloves, minced

1½ cups (260 g) cooked
black beans (or one
15-ounce/425-g can,
rinsed and drained)

Freshly ground black
pepper

¼ cup (60 ml) water or
vegetable broth

2 to 4 pasture-raised
eggs

vegan lime crema

1 cup (120 g) raw
cashews, soaked
overnight and drained

½ jalapeño, seeded and
chopped

1 teaspoon ground
cumin

1 garlic clove, minced

Pink salt

Juice of 1 to 2 limes

toppings

2 scallions, thinly sliced

Handful of cilantro

CFDC hot sauce (page
35) or store-bought hot
sauce (such as Cholula)

method

For the hash: Preheat the oven to 400°F (205°C). Line a baking sheet with parchment and toss the potatoes with half of the oil or ghee, half of the chili powder, and a few pinches of salt.

Roast the potatoes for 25 to 30 minutes, or until they are soft through and golden on the outside (cooking time will vary depending on the size of your cubes, so check their doneness before you take them out of the oven). Toss them once, halfway through.

Meanwhile, heat an ovenproof skillet or cast-iron pan over medium. Add the remaining oil or ghee and sauté the onion until soft, about 5 minutes. Add the garlic and the remaining chili powder and cook for 1 minute. Stir in the beans and season with salt and pepper. Add the water or broth to the pan and keep it warm over low heat. Once the potatoes are done roasting, add them to the beans and stir. Season with salt and pepper to taste.

Fill a saucepan two-thirds of the way with water, bring it to a boil, then reduce the heat to maintain a simmer. Crack an egg into a small cup and carefully slide it into the simmering water. Cook for 3 to 4 minutes, depending on how runny you like your yolk. Remove with a slotted spoon and gently place each egg on paper towels to drain.

For the lime crema: Blend the cashews, jalapeño, cumin, garlic, ½ teaspoon salt, the juice of one of the limes, and ¼ cup (60 ml) water in a blender or food processor until smooth. Thin with water as needed until it becomes a sour cream-like consistency. Season with additional lime and salt to taste. Refrigerate before serving. Store leftover crema for 3 to 4 days in the fridge.

To assemble the dish, divide the sweet potato hash into bowls. Top each serving with a poached egg, lime crema, scallions, cilantro, and hot sauce.

blueberry buckwheat pancakes

makes about 10 medium-size pancakes

ingredients

topping

1 cup (145 g) blueberries

1 cup (145 g) strawberries, sliced

Maple syrup

Juice and zest of 1 lemon

pancakes

1 cup (120 g) buckwheat flour

1 teaspoon baking powder

½ teaspoon baking soda

¼ teaspoon sea salt or pink salt

1 ripe banana

2 pasture-raised eggs (for vegan pancakes, see Note)

1 cup (240 ml) unsweetened vanilla almond milk (page 48)

Juice of 1 lemon

Coconut oil, for frying

When I first started cutting out gluten, my mind was hardwired to avoid anything that contained the word *wheat*. I can assure you that buckwheat *is* completely gluten free—it's actually a seed! Using buckwheat flour in this recipe results in a lighter and fluffier pancake. I use darker flour here, which makes the pancakes more fiber- and protein-rich and gives them a pretty purple hue. They're delicious plain, but stir a handful of blueberries into the batter, if you'd like. Make a big batch of these along with green smoothies (page 105) for an easy brunch with friends.

method

For the topping: combine the blueberries, strawberries, 1 tablespoon maple syrup, and as much of the lemon juice and zest as you like in a medium bowl. Adjust the amount of maple syrup to taste; set aside.

For the pancakes: Set the oven to a low heat for keeping the finished pancakes warm. In a large bowl, combine the buckwheat flour, baking powder, baking soda, and salt.

In a separate bowl, mash the banana and beat in the eggs, almond milk, and lemon juice. Pour the mixture into the bowl with the dry ingredients and mix until incorporated.

Heat some coconut oil in a pan over medium. Spoon about ¼ cup (60 ml) of the batter into the pan. Cook for 2 to 3 minutes on each side, then place the pancake in the oven to keep it warm. Repeat until you've used all the batter, adding coconut oil to the pan in between batches as needed.

Serve immediately with the fruit topping and additional maple syrup, if desired.

note:
Many recipes can be adapted for vegans using flax eggs: Whisk together 1 tablespoon ground flaxseed meal and 3 tablespoons water in place of each egg. Let sit for about 10 minutes, or until the mixture achieves a gelatinous, egglike consistency, then proceed as directed.

Unlike true wheats, buckwheat is low on the glycemic scale and helps balance your blood sugar. It's high in protein and fiber, which supports digestion, and keeps you full and energized longer. Buckwheat has a relatively high phytase content—the enzyme that helps break down those digestion disruptor phytates—so it's particularly effective when combined with grains that have low phytase content, like oats, because it will make them easier to digest. Try soaking and cooking your oats with buckwheat groats and see if you notice a difference!

Because of its slightly nutty and cinnamony flavor, buckwheat is one of my favorite gluten-free flours to use for baking, as in my mini carrot gingerbread muffins (page 170). Buckwheat flours differ in color—from light flour to a darker one. The darker flour will have a stronger taste, so experiment with what is available to you and decide which you prefer.

zucchini lasagna

serves 4

Vegan parm (page 38)

When you think of vegan lasagna, the fancy raw version comes to mind. Layers of pristinely stacked raw vegetables with sun-dried tomato sauce, cashew cream, and basil pesto. Yum. But beyond the layered look, it doesn't do much to evoke the true cheesy, baked lasagna of memory. This one is different. It's still packed with all the good-for-you veggies, but it feels decadent and nourishing. My classic tomato sauce and brazil nut ricotta make it taste so much like the real deal. When baked, the nut cream is completely transformed into a light, fluffy ricotta. This recipe requires a few more steps than most in this book, but it's worth it.

ingredients

3 mixed zucchini and yellow squash

3 small eggplant

2 tablespoons OmegaOil or oil of choice

Pink salt

Basic tomato sauce (recipe follows)

Brazil nut ricotta (recipe follows)

toppings

Vegan parm (page 38)

Small handful basil, torn

Pinch of red pepper flakes

Freshly ground black pepper

method

Preheat the oven to 350°F (175°C). Using a mandoline or sharp knife, thinly slice the squash and eggplant lengthwise into ⅛-inch-thick (3-mm) pieces. Brush both sides with oil and sprinkle with a pinch of salt.

Heat a grill pan over medium-high (see Note). When it's ready, working in batches, arrange the vegetable slices in a single layer on the pan and grill them for 2 minutes per side, or until they're cooked through and golden.

Arrange a layer of the zucchini and eggplant slices in the bottom of an 8-inch (20-cm) square baking dish, making sure they are slightly overlapping. Top with 1 cup (240 ml) of the tomato sauce, spreading it out evenly with the back of a spoon or spatula. Repeat with half of the ricotta. Add another layer of veggies, placing the veggies perpendicular to the first layer. Top with an additional layer of tomato sauce, then add the remaining ricotta. Finish with another layer of veggies. Bake the lasagna until it is warmed through and starting to bubble, 25 to 30 minutes.

Let the lasagna cool for 10 minutes before garnishing it with vegan parm, basil, red pepper flakes, and black pepper. Serve immediately.

note:
If you don't have a grill pan, you can use a nonstick skillet.

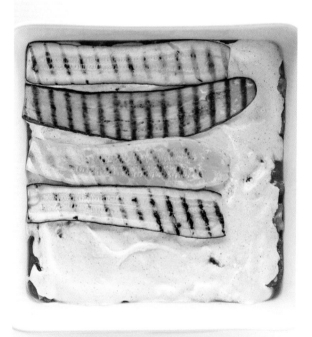

brazil nut ricotta

makes 1¼ cups (295 ml)

ingredients

½ cup (70 g) brazil nuts

½ cup (60 g) raw cashews

2 tablespoons nutritional yeast

Juice of 1 lemon

Sea salt or pink salt

Freshly ground black pepper

Pinch of red pepper flakes (optional)

method

Soak the brazil nuts and cashews in water overnight, or for at least 8 hours. Rinse and drain them, then puree them with the yeast, lemon juice, ½ teaspoon salt, black pepper, red pepper flakes (if you're using them), and ½ cup (120 ml) filtered water, 1 tablespoon at a time, in a blender or food processor. If needed, add more water to adjust the consistency and add a pinch more salt to taste.

note:

This is also great dolloped and baked on pizzas and flatbreads (page 88) when adding the other toppings.

basic tomato sauce

makes 3 cups (705 ml)

ingredients

5 ripe beefsteak tomatoes
(about 2 pounds/910 g)

1 tablespoon OmegaOil or oil of choice

1 onion, chopped

2 garlic cloves, minced

Sea salt or pink salt

Juice of ½ lemon

Small handful of torn fresh basil

method

Boil a large pot of water and prep an ice bath by filling a large bowl with water and ice and setting it nearby.

Prepare the tomatoes for blanching by cutting a very shallow X in the bottom of each one. Place them in the boiling water and cook for about 1 minute. Use tongs or a slotted spoon to lift them out and plunge them into the ice bath.

Once they have cooled, peel away the skin, core out the stem with a small paring knife, and roughly chop them. Set them aside in a bowl.

Bring a pan to medium-high and add the oil. Once it's warm, add the onions and sauté until they are soft and translucent, 5 to 7 minutes. Add the garlic and sauté for 30 to 60 seconds.

Add the tomatoes, a generous pinch of salt, and the fresh lemon juice, and simmer over low for 20 to 30 minutes. Turn off the heat and stir in the basil.

Use the sauce immediately or store it in an airtight container in the fridge for 3 to 4 days, or up to 3 months in the freezer.

note:

Keep tomato sauce on hand for easy prep. I like to double the recipe so I'll have extra to use on spaghetti squash, pasta, or zucchini noodles for quick dinners the rest of the week!

flatbread with brussels sprouts, corn + caramelized onion

makes 2 personal-size flatbreads

In the early days of being gluten-free, pizza more flavorful than cardboard could be hard to come by, so I decided to make my own. Each pizza crust combo resulted in a wildly different texture and flavor: from a frittata-leaning cauliflower crust to a sweeter but more familiar "pizza" texture in a sweet potato crust. In the end, the flatbread won me over. The combo of chickpea flour and oat flour yields a hearty crust that stands on its own in flavor but doesn't overpower the toppings. You'll make any pizza lover (gluten-free or not) happy.

ingredients

caramelized onions

1 tablespoon OmegaOil or oil of choice

1 red onion, thinly sliced

Pink salt or sea salt

pizza dough

¾ cup (180 ml) warm water

1 teaspoon maple syrup

1 packet instant yeast (or 2¼ teaspoons/7g)

1 cup (90 g) chickpea flour

½ cup plus 2 tablespoons (55 g) oat flour

¼ cup (30 g) arrowroot powder

2 tablespoons psyllium husks

1 teaspoon sea salt or pink salt

1 tablespoon OmegaOil or oil of choice, plus more for the parchment

brussels sprouts + corn

1 tablespoon OmegaOil or oil of choice

10 Brussels sprouts, trimmed, cut in half crosswise, and thinly sliced

Kernels from 2 ears of corn

Sea salt or pink salt

Freshly ground black pepper

toppings

CFDC pesto (page 37)

2 handfuls of arugula

Red pepper flakes (optional)

method

For the caramelized onions: heat a small skillet over medium. Add the oil and when it shimmers, add the onion. Stir well to coat, add a pinch of salt, and turn the heat to low. Stir occasionally, until onions are caramelized, about 30 minutes. Set them aside.

For the dough: In a large mixing bowl, combine the warm water and maple syrup. Sprinkle the yeast on top and let sit for 10 minutes.

In a separate bowl, stir together the chickpea and oat flours, the arrowroot, psyllium, and salt. Add the wet ingredients and the oil to this mixture and mix well. This should yield a slightly sticky dough that easily pulls away from the side of the bowl. If it's too wet, add one tablespoon of oat flour at a time. Cover the bowl with a large plate and let rise for 45 minutes.

Preheat the oven to 425°F (220°C) and place an inverted baking sheet on a rack in the bottom third of your oven. Let the oven preheat for at least 30 minutes.

Once the dough has risen, roll out a sheet of parchment paper the length of a baking sheet. Lightly coat with oil and divide the dough into two pieces. Drop each piece on either side of the parchment, and drizzle a bit more oil on top of each. Use your hands to gently press the dough out toward the edges of the parchment,

forming two flatbreads. Let rise for an additional 10 minutes. Meanwhile, trim the parchment to frame each flatbread by about an inch.

Brush the tops of the dough lightly with oil and slip onto the inverted baking sheet in the oven (keeping them on the parchment). Bake the dough for 5 minutes. After 5 minutes, use a fork to prick the top of the crust several times, then bake it for an additional 3 to 5 minutes.

While the flatbread is baking, heat a medium skillet over medium. Add the oil and when it shimmers, add the Brussels sprouts and corn. Mix well, adding a generous pinch of salt and pepper. Cook until the Brussels sprouts are browned, about 10 minutes. Season to taste.

Top the crust with a thin layer of pesto. Add the caramelized onions and a generous amount of the Brussels sprouts mixture. Bake the topped dough for 5 to 7 minutes, or until the crust turns golden brown. Top with fresh arugula and a pinch of red pepper flakes, if desired.

spaghetti squash + mushroom meatballs

makes about 30 meatballs; serves 4 to 6

<u>note:</u>
If the spaghetti squash is difficult to cut, you can pop the whole squash in the oven—you will just need to cook it about 30 minutes longer. Once the whole squash is cooked through, let cool for 5 minutes or until you can touch it comfortably. Carefully cut it in half (the steam coming out will be hot!), and proceed as usual.

Spaghetti squash is magical, and you don't need any fancy gadgets for this one. Once it's cooked, you'll use a fork to gently pull the spaghetti-like strands out of their shell. It's insane how good this is, thanks to the mushrooms' texture and versatility, the bite from the almonds, the heat from the red pepper flakes, and the brightness from the lemon and fresh herbs. If you have leftover "meatballs," try them in veggie bowls or on brown rice pasta with a fried egg.

ingredients

1 spaghetti squash

OmegaOil or oil of choice

1 small yellow onion, diced

2 garlic cloves, minced

8 ounces (225 g) cremini mushrooms, cleaned with a dry towel and sliced

½ cup (45 g) gluten-free rolled oats

½ cup (55 g) chopped raw almonds

1½ cups (275 g) cooked cannellini beans (or one 15-ounce/425-g can, rinsed and drained)

½ teaspoon freshly ground black pepper

Generous pinch of red pepper flakes

Juice of ½ lemon

½ cup (20 g) basil, chopped

¼ cup (13 g) flat-leaf parsley, chopped

Sea salt or pink salt

Serve with: basic tomato sauce (page 87) or CFDC pesto (page 37)

Vegan parm (page 38)

method

Preheat the oven to 375°F (190°C). Line a baking dish and a baking sheet with parchment paper and set them aside.

Carefully cut the spaghetti squash in half and scrape out the seeds using a spoon (see Note, opposite). Place the halves face down in the prepared baking dish, and bake for 30 to 45 minutes or until tender (you should be able to pierce it all the way though with a fork). Remove the halves from the oven and let them cool slightly. Use a fork to gently pull the flesh of the squash away from the skin to form noodle-like strands. Keep warm.

While the squash bakes, heat a medium skillet over medium. Once it's hot, add 1 tablespoon oil and the onion and cook for 5 minutes. Add the garlic and mushrooms and cook for another 2 minutes, until the vegetables are soft but just barely cooked. Pour the mixture into a fine-mesh strainer and set it aside over a bowl or pot for 5 minutes. This will drain all the excess liquid so your meatball mixture isn't too wet.

In a food processor, pulse the rolled oats and almonds until they become a rough flour (it's okay if there are some larger pieces). Add the beans, black pepper, red pepper flakes, lemon juice, basil, parsley, and 1 teaspoon salt; pulse until the ingredients are incorporated. Add the mushroom mixture to the food processor and pulse until it forms a chunky puree. Taste and adjust the seasoning as needed (I usually add a few more pinches of salt). Let the mixture sit at room temperature for about 10 minutes.

Use a tablespoon-size cookie scoop to place the mushroom mixture on the prepared baking sheet. If you don't have a cookie scoop, measure out a scant tablespoon and pat the mixture into a ball using your hands. It should hold together easily, although you will have to shape it very gently. Repeat with the remaining mixture, arranging the balls on the prepared baking sheet with plenty of space between them. Lightly brush the tops with oil and bake for 30 minutes, gently flipping them over halfway through. When they are done, the meatballs will be lightly browned and slightly firm to the touch.

Serve the meatballs on top of the spaghetti squash, along with basic tomato sauce or pesto and vegan parm.

weeknight chili

serves 4 to 6

This chili can be prepared in about 30 minutes, making it relatively quick to whip up. The kidney and black beans offer a double punch of plant-based iron, fiber, and protein. In colder months, you can swap out the zucchini for 2 cups (300 g) of butternut squash or sweet potato, which will yield an even heartier, slightly sweeter chili.

ingredients

2 tablespoons coconut oil or ghee

1 yellow onion, diced

3 large carrots, diced

3 stalks celery, diced

2 large bell peppers (red, orange, or yellow), seeded and diced

2 garlic cloves, minced

1 tablespoon chili powder, or to taste

½ teaspoon sea salt or pink salt, or to taste

½ teaspoon dried oregano

⅛ teaspoon cayenne, or to taste

2 zucchini or summer squash, thinly sliced

1 cup (240 ml) tomato sauce (or one 8-ounce/227-g can)

1½ cups (265 g) cooked red kidney beans (or one 15-ounce/425-g can, rinsed and drained)

1½ cups (260 g) cooked black beans (or one 15-ounce/425-g can, rinsed and drained)

1 dried bay leaf

toppings

Leaves from 1 bunch cilantro, roughly chopped

Scallions, thinly sliced

Several sprouted corn tortillas, cut into ¼-inch (6-mm) strips and toasted (see Note)

Lime wedges

Vegan lime crema (page 81) and classic guac (page 118)

method

Heat the oil in a large Dutch oven or heavy-bottomed pot over medium. Add the onion, carrots, celery, and bell peppers and cook for about 10 minutes, until the veggies start to soften. Try not to stir frequently, as you want the veggies to caramelize rather than steam. Add the garlic along with the chili powder, salt, oregano, and cayenne. Cook for 2 more minutes.

Add the zucchini, tomato sauce, kidney and black beans, and ½ cup (120 ml) water along with the bay leaf. Bring the chili to a rolling boil, then reduce the heat to low. Taste and adjust the seasonings as desired. For additional spice, add a dash more cayenne pepper; for a richer flavor, a dash of chili powder.

Cover and cook on low for 20 to 25 minutes, allowing the flavors to marry. Remove the bay leaf and again adjust seasoning as needed.

Serve topped with cilantro, scallions, a dollop each of lime crema and guac, and a pile of toasted corn tortilla strips.

note:
To toast the tortillas, preheat the oven to 375°F (190°C). Spread the tortilla strips out on a small pan and bake until crispy, about 10 minutes. Let them cool for 5 minutes before serving.

sesame noodle bowls with pan-fried tofu

serves 4

Noodle bowls are ideal because they don't use too many pots and pans, and leftovers make the perfect lunch the next day. This one ups the veggie factor and removes all the refined, white sugars usually hidden in noodles and dressing. We're going for the good stuff here—you can use either soba (buckwheat) noodles or brown rice and sweet potato noodles. If you're using the soba noodles, make sure they are 100 percent buckwheat if you're gluten free, as many are cut with wheat flour. The sesame dressing is the perfect balance of sweet and sour, and the pan-fried tofu caramelizes with pieces of crispy ginger. You will seriously want to top everything with this tofu, and dare I say it, it may just be the best you've ever had.

ingredients

1 (8.8-ounce/250-g) package soba noodles or brown rice and sweet potato noodles, such as King Soba

sesame dressing

3 tablespoons low-sodium gluten-free tamari

2 tablespoons sesame oil

2 tablespoons olive oil

2 tablespoons apple cider vinegar

½ teaspoon coconut sugar or honey

Pinch of red pepper flakes

Squeeze of lime

1 tablespoon CFDC hot sauce (page 35; optional)

pan-fried tofu

2 tablespoons low-sodium gluten-free tamari

½ tablespoon apple cider vinegar

1 teaspoon honey

1 teaspoon grated, peeled fresh ginger

1 garlic clove, minced

1 tablespoon coconut oil

1 teaspoon sesame oil

1 (16-ounce/455-g) package extra-firm organic tofu, drained and cut into 1-inch (2.5-cm) cubes

other additions

3 zucchini, peeled, shredded or spiralized, and blotted dry

4 scallions, thinly sliced, plus more for garnish

2 small red bell peppers, seeded and cut into matchsticks

4 large handfuls of spinach, roughly chopped

¼ cup (35 g) tamari almonds (page 39)

method

For the dressing: In a small bowl, whisk together all the ingredients for the sesame dressing and set it aside.

Bring a pot of water to boil and cook the noodles according to the package directions.

For the tofu: Combine the tamari, apple cider vinegar, honey, ginger, and garlic and set aside. Heat the coconut and sesame oils over medium in a medium skillet (see Note). Once the oil is shimmering, add the tofu. Do not stir! Let the tofu cubes cook for 2 to 3 minutes and flip them to the other side. Cook for an additional 2 minutes, until both sides are browned. Add the tamari mixture, turn the heat to low, and stir the tofu until it is well coated in the sauce. Set aside.

Combine the noodles with the zucchini, bell peppers, and scallions. Add the sesame dressing and toss to combine. Serve on a large platter or in individual bowls topped with the tofu, spinach, tamari almonds, and additional scallions.

note:
For best results when cooking tofu, use a nonstick skillet. Look for heavy-bottomed ceramic-coated pans when purchasing a nonstick pan, and be sure to use wooden cooking utensils, as metal can scrape the finish off the pan.

lentil tacos with simple slaw + corn avocado salsa

serves 4

Lentils are packed with folic acid, which can help naturally increase serotonin levels, our "happy" mood-boosting hormone. Here they are paired with a slightly spicy, yet tangy salsa and crunchy cabbage. I serve them on sprouted corn tortillas, which are rather sturdy and hold up to the weight of the lentils without breaking. Another bonus—sprouted corn is easier to digest and more nutrient-rich. I love the way it tastes, but you can always sub regular corn tortillas.

ingredients

taco filling

1 tablespoon OmegaOil or oil of choice

1 yellow onion, diced

Sea salt or pink salt

2 large garlic cloves, minced

1 teaspoon chili powder

½ teaspoon ground cumin

1 cup (190 g) brown lentils, picked over for debris and rinsed

2 cups (480 ml) vegetable broth or water

corn avocado salsa

1 avocado, diced

1 cup (140 g) fresh or frozen corn (kernels from about 2 ears)

¼ cup (30 g) diced red onion

½ jalapeño, seeded and finely diced

¼ cup (10 g) chopped cilantro

Juice of 1 lime, plus more to taste

Sea salt or pink salt to taste

for serving

1 (10-ounce/280 g) package sprouted corn tortillas

Simple slaw (page 41)

Vegan lime crema (page 81)

method

For the filling: Heat the oil in a medium pot over medium. Add the onion and a pinch of salt and cook for 5 to 7 minutes, until the pieces are softened. Add the garlic, chili powder, and cumin, and sauté for another minute, stirring constantly. Add the lentils and broth. Raise the heat to medium-high and bring the mixture to a gentle simmer, reducing the heat as needed to maintain it. Cook, partially covered, for 25 minutes. Remove the lid and continue simmering for 5 to 10 minutes, until the lentils are cooked through and the liquid has nearly evaporated.

Check the lentils for doneness—they should be soft but retain a slight tooth. If the liquid has evaporated but the lentils aren't cooked through, add another splash. Drain off any excess liquid once the lentils are done and lightly mash some of them together.

For the salsa: Combine all the ingredients and stir. Adjust the seasonings to taste. Set aside.

For the tortillas: Heat a large nonstick skillet over medium. Place a tortilla in the skillet and warm it for about 30 seconds per side. If it is a bit stiff from the fridge, use your fingers to spritz it with a little water before placing it in the pan. This will make it softer, and it will heat through faster. Place the warmed tortilla in a clean folded kitchen towel until you're ready to serve. Repeat with the remaining tortillas.

For serving, create a taco assembly line, piling the tortillas with lentils, salsa, simple slaw, and lime crema.

peaches + raw brazil nut crumble

serves 4

This summer dessert is actually good for you *and* your skin. Peaches are filled with collagen-boosting vitamin C and the antioxidant lutein, which supports healthy skin and eyes. I love serving this with a coconut yogurt or ice cream, which pairs perfectly with the peach (think of your classic Creamsicle, only deconstructed and peachy). I keep it on the lighter side for summer by topping it with a raw crumble filled with nutrient-dense brazil nuts.

ingredients

baked peaches

4 peaches, cut in half and pitted

1 tablespoon balsamic vinegar

Drizzle of raw honey (optional)

raw crumble

½ cup (70 g) brazil nuts

5 to 6 pitted medjool dates

½ teaspoon ground cinnamon

Sea salt or pink salt

4 scoops of coconut yogurt or coconut ice cream (optional)

method

For the peaches: Preheat the oven to 350°F (175°C). Drizzle the peaches with the balsamic vinegar and honey, if you're using it. Place them facedown in a parchment-lined baking dish or small sheet pan. Bake for 35 to 40 minutes, until they're softened and lightly browned.

Meanwhile, make the raw crumble: Place all of the ingredients in a food processor and pulse until the nuts become large crumbs. The mixture should hold together when you pinch it.

Serve the peaches with lots of crumble on top and a big dollop of coconut yogurt or coconut ice cream, if desired.

Go (BRAZIL) NUTS

Brazil nuts are filled with healthy fats, making them an amazing skin and brain food. They are *insanely* high in the essential trace mineral selenium, most often found in seafood, which is critical for cognitive function and a healthy immune system. Even just one or two nuts can provide your daily dose. They also contain a bevy of other immune-boosting nutrients like zinc and magnesium. Magnesium is nature's relaxation and antianxiety tool, and it helps your muscles relax.

So if you haven't gone nuts yet, it's time to jump on the wagon. Opt for raw brazil nuts (sans roasting and salt) and blend them into a creamy milk to enjoy alone or in a smoothie. I also love combining them with other nuts—to make homemade nut butters or cheeses, as in my veggie lasagna (page 84).

avocado

coconut mint
hair treatment

rosemary

coconut + peppermint oils

coconut mint hair treatment

makes 1 treatment

This naturally moisturizing hair mask is packed with hydrating, antibacterial ingredients that are great for dry hair. If your hair is fine or tends to be oily, give it a second wash after the treatment or apply it only to the ends of your hair. While you're all wrapped up, double up with a brightening green tea mask (page 175) or healing honey face mask (page 149). You're all set for the perfect spa night in.

AVOCADO
is moisturizing and rich in vitamin E, which can help strengthen hair and improve growth.

COCONUT OIL
is hydrating, antibacterial, and antifungal.

ROSEMARY
is antibacterial and helps improve circulation to the scalp.

PEPPERMINT
is invigorating, helps improve circulation to the scalp, and smells amazing!

ingredients

¼ avocado

2 tablespoons coconut oil, melted

Leaves from 1 sprig of rosemary, finely minced

20 drops peppermint oil

method

Mash the avocado, coconut oil, rosemary, and peppermint oil together. Mix until it is super creamy so that it will blend into your hair easily. Brush your hair out and apply the mixture starting at the roots and working down toward the ends of your hair. Cover your hair with an old towel (or a piece of plastic wrap) and leave the treatment on for 30 minutes. Shampoo and condition as usual.

Note: This recipe yields enough for one treatment on medium-length, thick hair. If your hair is very thick and long, double the recipe. The mask will keep in the fridge for a few days, so you can make enough at one time to use it two days in a row for an extra-intense treatment. While this mask shouldn't stain your towels, I wouldn't use your pristine white towels or any that you care about. I use an old hand towel and clip the bottom of it together to keep it securely on my head.

detox

You know the sluggish, overstuffed feeling that can roll in after an overindulgent holiday season, vacation, or just the weekend? There's actually something you can do about it to get you from 0 to 100—stat. The key is lots of anti-inflammatory whole foods that will support your body's natural detoxification process and get you back on track.

Detox has become a buzzword over the last few years, and if you think these recipes are all smoothies and juices, you might be surprised. Yes, there is a super green smoothie recipe packed full of alkalizing green veggies (it's impossible to not include a green smoothie in this chapter!), but you'll also find a warming, minestrone soup, roasted vegetable quinoa salads, and beet berry pops. Green vegetables come through as the star in this chapter—they are super detoxifiers that support just about every function in your body.

Make sure to saturate your body with nutrient-dense foods on a detox—you should never feel deprived. If you are starving when you are in a detox mood, eat more and fill your plate with healthy fats, like avocados and seeds, or lean proteins. The best part about these recipes is that they are truly ones you can revisit every day. They're meant to be used in tandem—as a full detox—or on their own, as part of lunches and dinners with recipes from other chapters in this book. Like many of my recipes, they fully let your body relax and reset from the inside out.

super green smoothie

makes 1 smoothie

Most days, I'm a smoothie over juice type of gal. Smoothies contain fiber, keeping you full and satisfied, and your blood sugar happy. Juices can contain a lot of sugar, and without the fiber to balance it all out, they can cause a spike in blood sugar. Best to leave the fiber in! This is a tropical take on my classic green smoothie. It's refreshing, hydrating, and rich in greens. Dark, leafy greens and cilantro are both detoxifying and cancer-fighting, and the cucumber and coconut water are hydrating, to nourish every cell in your body. Enjoy morning, afternoon, or even poolside.

ingredients

1 cup (240 ml) raw coconut water

2 handfuls of dark, leafy greens (like spinach or kale)

1 small Persian cucumber, or a 2-inch (5-cm) piece of a large cucumber

½ cup (125 g) frozen pineapple chunks

½-inch (12-mm) piece fresh ginger, peeled

3 sprigs of cilantro

1 teaspoon coconut oil

Squeeze of lime

A few cubes of ice

method

Puree all the ingredients together in a blender until completely smooth.

the evergreen bowl

serves 2

This bowl is light on its own, full of green vegetables (the building blocks of any good detox), but you can easily add beans, pan-fried tofu (page 94), or a poached egg for an extra kick of protein.

ingredients

3 cups bite-size pieces of mixed green vegetables (broccoli florets, zucchini, snap peas, asparagus, green beans)

1 cup (185 g) cooked quinoa

2 radishes, thinly sliced

1 avocado, halved and thinly sliced

2 teaspoons sesame seeds

Handful of sprouts or microgreens

2 tablespoons tamari almonds (page 39) or raw almonds

Cilantro detox dressing (recipe follows)

method

Bring a large pot of water to a simmer and blanch the vegetables for 2 to 3 minutes. (You want them to turn bright green and be just cooked, but still have bite to them.)

Drain well and serve the vegetables over the quinoa with radishes, avocado, sesame seeds, sprouts, and almonds. Drizzle on the cilantro detox dressing.

cilantro detox dressing

makes 1 cup (240 ml)

ingredients

2 cups (60 g) cilantro

1 garlic clove

½-inch (12-mm) piece fresh ginger, peeled

1 tablespoon chopped jalapeño (less or more depending on your heat tolerance)

Sea salt or pink salt

Juice of 1 lemon

½ to ¾ cup (120 to 180 ml) olive oil

method

Combine the cilantro, garlic, ginger, jalapeño, lemon, and ¼ teaspoon salt in a blender or food processor and puree until well combined. Slowly drizzle in the oil until the mixture reaches a pourable consistency. Season with additional salt to taste.

mom's minestrone

serves 4

Warming and cooked foods have their place in a detox—it's not just about raw foods. They are incredibly healing and require less work from your body to digest, so it can focus more on the natural detoxification process. This minestrone is a take on what my mom made for me growing up—a big bowl makes me feel deeply comforted and lets my body know that it's okay to let go and relax.

ingredients

1 tablespoon ghee or oil of choice

1 yellow onion, chopped

2 carrots, chopped

2 stalks celery, chopped

1 garlic clove, minced

1 teaspoon dried oregano

1 teaspoon dried basil

4 cups (960 ml) vegan bone broth (page 52)

2 cups (230 g) butternut squash, cut into ½-inch (12-mm) cubes

1 large tomato, chopped

1 zucchini, halved lengthwise and cut into half-moons (optional)

2 cups (360 g) cooked white beans (or one 15-ounce/425-g can, rinsed and drained)

2 handfuls of greens (spinach, kale, or chard), roughly chopped

Sea salt or pink salt

Freshly ground black pepper

Chopped flat-leaf parsley, for garnish

method

In a large heavy-bottomed pot, heat the ghee or oil over medium-high. Add the onion, carrots, and celery and sauté, stirring occasionally until the onion is translucent, 5 to 7 minutes. Add the garlic and sauté for an additional minute. Add the oregano and basil and sauté until fragrant, about 30 seconds.

Add the broth, squash, and tomato. Bring the mixture to a boil, then reduce the heat to low and simmer the soup, partially covered, until the squash is nearly cooked through, about 15 minutes. Add the zucchini, if using, and the beans; cook for 5 minutes.

Remove the soup from the heat, stir in the greens, and season with salt and pepper to taste. Garnish with parsley and serve immediately.

The minestrone will keep in the fridge for up to 4 days, or up to 3 months in the freezer.

arugula + roots salad

serves 4 to 6 as a side

I love eating with the seasons—but what should you do during those dark winter days when you are craving something fresh, colorful, and uplifting? Enter this instantly refreshing and mood-lifting salad. The root vegetables provide a satisfying crunch, and the watermelon radishes add a nice pop of color. Plus, both are high in vitamin C and are detoxifying and supportive for your liver. This salad is perfect for daytime parties and casual lunches with friends (see my go-to ladies' lunch spread on pages 208–209).

ingredients

lemon dressing

2 tablespoons olive oil

Juice of 1 lemon

1 teaspoon raw honey

Sea salt or pink salt

Freshly ground black pepper

salad

¼ cup (30 g) hazelnuts

2 watermelon radishes, thinly sliced

1 golden beet, peeled and thinly sliced

8 large handfuls of arugula

Handful of torn mint

2 teaspoons bee pollen

method

For the dressing: whisk together the oil, lemon juice, and honey. Add the salt and pepper to taste and set aside.

For the salad: Preheat the oven to 350°F (175°C). Line a baking sheet with parchment and toast the hazelnuts in the oven for 10 minutes, watching carefully to be sure they don't burn. Rub skins off in a kitchen towel and allow the nuts to cool. Coarsely chop.

Use a mandoline to thinly slice the watermelon radishes and golden beet. Toss with the arugula, half of the mint, half of the hazelnuts, and the lemon dressing. Garnish with the remaining hazelnuts and mint, and the bee pollen.

just BEET it

Beets are a humble root vegetable that clean house in major ways. They are great supporters of the liver; their phytochemicals spur liver function and help both process and eliminate toxins. Beets are also high in antioxidants and iron, making them anti-inflammatory and blood-purifying.

There are a few different varieties of beets, from red to golden to Chioggia. I love the red beets but often opt for other varieties in salads when I don't want to stain everything red! You may be surprised that beets can be eaten raw—they are actually delicious when shaved thin or grated into small pieces. They are also a nice addition to smoothies, juices, and veggie burgers. Don't use just the root: Sauté the leaves or use them in juices; and add the skins of golden beets to veggie broths, which results in a slightly sweet, well-rounded broth.

pesto zucchini noodles

serves 4

This dish epitomizes August on the East Coast. I love pairing peak-of-the-season tomatoes with fresh, bright basil pesto, all tangled together with zucchini noodles. Before tossing the pasta, I slow roast the tomatoes—it's like having the sun kiss them all over again. The result is the sweetest, most flavorful treat and a perfect dish to keep you feeling light and refreshed during the warm summer months. Enjoy these noodles as is—soaking in the season—or pair them with lentil salads and grilled vegetables like eggplant. Top your bowl with vegan parm, if you'd like, and dig in.

ingredients

1 pint (10 ounces/280 g) mixed cherry tomatoes

1 tablespoon olive oil

Sea salt or pink salt

4 to 6 mixed zucchini and summer squash, spiralized or julienne peeled

CFDC pesto (page 37)

Vegan parm (optional, page 38)

method

Preheat the oven to 250°F (120°C) and line a baking sheet with parchment paper. Toss the tomatoes with olive oil and a generous pinch of salt. Bake them for 30 to 40 minutes, or until the tomatoes shine and look like they are about to burst.

Toss the zucchini noodles with a generous amount of pesto. Gently stir in half of the tomatoes. Serve with the remaining tomatoes on top and an additional topping of vegan parm if desired.

squash + sprouts kale salad

serves 2 as a main, 4 as a side

ingredients

sesame-ginger dressing

2 tablespoons low-sodium gluten-free tamari

Juice of 1 lime

2 teaspoons apple cider vinegar

1-inch (2.5-cm) piece fresh ginger, peeled and finely grated

1 garlic clove, finely grated (optional)

¼ cup (60 ml) toasted sesame oil

Sea salt or pink salt

Freshly ground black pepper

salad

1 delicata squash, cut lengthwise, seeded, and sliced into ⅛-inch (3-mm) half-moons

10 to 12 Brussels sprouts, trimmed and halved

2 tablespoons OmegaOil or oil of choice

Sea salt or pink salt

Freshly ground black pepper

1 bunch of kale (such as Tuscan or purple)

¼ cup (35 g) pepitas, toasted

I'm a lover of kale salads. Yes, they are trendy, but they're here to stay. Done right, kale salads not only pack a nutritional punch, but they also are hearty enough to stand as a meal on their own. Plus, kale has been crowned the queen of vegetables when it comes to nutritional benefits. This dish, with its Asian-inspired dressing and my all-time favorite (bright yellow!) squash, ensures that I (and hopefully you!) won't be getting sick of kale anytime soon.

method

For the dressing: In a small bowl, whisk together the tamari, lime juice, vinegar, ginger, garlic, and sesame oil until they are well combined. Taste and season with salt and pepper as needed. Set aside.

For the salad: Preheat the oven to 400°F (205°C) and line a baking sheet with parchment paper. Drizzle the squash and Brussels sprouts with oil and toss them with salt and pepper until they're well coated. Place the Brussels sprouts on the baking sheet with the cut side facing down so they get nice and golden. Spread the squash out on the sheet as well. Roast the vegetables for 25 to 30 minutes or until the squash and sprouts are cooked through and golden.

Meanwhile, trim the kale and remove the stems. Roughly chop and place the kale into a large bowl. Add a pinch of salt and gently massage it into the kale using your hands. Toss the kale with a couple of tablespoons of the dressing and set the salad aside.

Remove the veggies from the oven, and let them cool for 5 minutes before tossing them with the kale and more dressing as needed. Top the salad with the pepitas before serving.

hail to KALE

Kale's claim to fame is that, calorie for calorie, it has more iron than beef. In fact, it's one of the most nutrient-dense foods on earth. It's full of antioxidants and fiber, and has nutrients that fight against inflammation and cancer. Like other cruciferous vegetables, it contains sulfur, making it a super detox veggie. It's also rich in vitamin K, which can help strengthen bones and prevent osteoporosis.

Raw kale can be tough and dense (meaning very fibrous—which is also a reason we love it!), so I recommend giving it a nice massage if you are enjoying it raw. After a minute or so of massaging, the leaves will start to break down and become less tough. Kale has a number of varieties to choose from, such as curly kale, purple kale, and Tuscan kale. All three are perfect for salads. Curly and purple kale are great steamed, or as kale chips, and Tuscan is delicious in pesto or stirred into soups. I also use baby kale, which is good for blending into smoothies and is less bitter than the others. Play around to find out which variety is your favorite!

cfdc chopped salad + creamy avocado dressing

serves 2 generously

This chopped salad is an "everything but the kitchen sink" salad. It's endlessly customizable, which is good because—even in detox mode—who wants to eat the same exact salad every day? Toss together a few veggies, proteins, some crunch, and a creamy dressing, and you're good to go. When it comes to veggies here, the more the merrier. Prep some of these ingredients on Sunday, and you can switch up your salad routine all week long.

ingredients

creamy avocado dressing

½ avocado

2 tablespoons minced shallot

1 garlic clove, pressed

Juice of 1½ lemons

¼ cup (10 g) chopped fresh herbs such as cilantro, parsley, basil, chives, or mint

¼ cup (60 ml) unsweetened almond milk (page 48)

Sea salt or pink salt

⅓ cup (75 ml) olive oil

Freshly ground black pepper

for the salad base:

1 head romaine, chopped

choose at least 4 of the following:

1 carrot, grated

½ English cucumber, sliced into half-moons

1 red, yellow, or orange bell pepper, seeded and chopped

½ cup (55 g) bite-size pieces green beans, blanched

½ cup (55 g) snap peas, blanched

½ cup (65 g) bite-size pieces asparagus, blanched

½ cup (75 g) cherry tomatoes, halved

1 medium beet (red or golden), chopped

choose 1 of these pairs:

Black beans + avocado

Lentils + toasted pepitas

Chickpeas + pasture-raised hard-boiled eggs

Quinoa + toasted slivered almonds

optional toppings:

Hemp hearts

Sprouts

Cilantro, parsley, basil, scallions, chives, or mint

method

For the dressing: In a blender or food processor, combine the avocado, shallot, garlic, lemon juice, herbs, almond milk, and a pinch of salt; blend until smooth. Slowly add the olive oil. If needed, add water to thin to your desired consistency. Season to taste with additional salt, as needed, and black pepper. Set aside.

For the salad: In a large bowl, combine the romaine with your choices of vegetables and pairings. Toss the salad with the dressing until it is lightly coated. Add your desired toppings and serve with additional dressing on the side.

classic guac + jicama with lime + chili

serves 4

During warmer weather in NYC, you can find people on busy street corners cutting mangoes into perfect slices and topping them with lime and chili for hungry pedestrians. This snack inspired me to sprinkle lime and chili on just about everything, including jicama. Jicama is a round, funny-looking root vegetable with thick, brown skin that must be peeled. Once peeled, it's crunchy, juicy, and surprisingly refreshing. It's crisp like an apple but leans savory like a turnip. Look for this fiber-rich, low-glycemic tuber at your local grocery store, and pair it with one of my all-time favorite recipes for guacamole.

ingredients

guacamole

3 Hass avocados

1 Roma tomato, finely chopped

½ red onion, finely chopped

1 jalapeño, veins and seeds removed, chopped

Juice of 1 or 2 limes to taste

1 small bunch of cilantro, roughly chopped

Sea salt or pink salt

jicama with lime + chili

1 jicama, peeled and cut into matchsticks

Juice of 1 lime

A few pinches of chili powder

method

For the guacamole, halve the avocados and remove the pits and skin. Put them in the food processor and add the tomato, onion, jalapeño, some of the lime juice, and the cilantro; pulse until the mixture is nearly smooth. (If you prefer a chunkier guacamole, pulse less, or mash everything together in a large bowl, as pictured.) Taste and season with salt and additional lime juice as needed.

In a medium bowl, toss the jicama, lime juice, and chili powder together and serve with the guac!

green goodness dip

makes about 2 cups (480 ml)

ingredients

Sea salt or pink salt

Assorted vegetables such as asparagus, carrots, cauliflower, and beans, cut into roughly uniform pieces for dipping

1 head garlic, roasted (see page 37)

2 handfuls of spinach

2 tablespoons chives, plus more for topping

Juice of ½ lemon, plus more as needed

1 teaspoon red pepper flakes

2 cups (365 g) cooked cannellini beans (or one 15-ounce/425-g can, rinsed and drained)

Freshly ground black pepper

¼ cup (60 ml) extra-virgin olive oil

I'm always looking for new ways to pack in my greens, especially during snack time. Here I've snuck in fresh spinach to make this dip full of green goodness and give it a beautiful hue. Briefly blanching the vegetables makes them easier to digest, brighter, and more flavorful. You can also enjoy this dip with flax crackers or as a spread in wraps and sandwiches.

method

Decide which of your chosen vegetables you wish to serve raw and which you plan to blanch. Set the raw vegetables aside. Prepare a large ice bath and set aside a plate lined with a kitchen or paper towel. Bring a large pot of water to boil. Salt the water once it is boiling.

In small batches, add the blanching vegetables to the pot. The water should continue to boil while they cook, 2 to 4 minutes per batch. Taste the veggies for doneness by removing one with a slotted spoon and quickly cooling it in the ice water.

Once they are cooked, remove the veggies with a slotted spoon and plunge them into the ice bath until they are completely cooled. Transfer them to the prepared plate to dry.

For the dip: In a food processor, combine the roasted garlic, spinach, chives, lemon juice, and red pepper flakes. Pulse until well combined. Add the beans, ¼ teaspoon salt, and black pepper to taste. Pulse a few times and then drizzle the olive oil into the mixture while continuing to pulse until the dip is smooth. Taste and adjust with a pinch of salt or a squeeze of lemon if needed.

Serve the dip with the mixture of raw and blanched veggies.

beach quinoa salad

serves 4

I have a Memorial Day tradition with my girlfriends from home where we head down to the beaches on the Eastern Shore in Delaware. It hasn't always been known to be the healthiest weekend, there are more grapefruit crushes than green juices. But still, we make sure to stock the fridge with light, refreshing, satisfying options, and that's where this quinoa salad comes in. The quinoa and chickpeas make for a hearty salad and a good source of protein. Quinoa is anti-inflammatory, full of antioxidants, and easy to digest—so no bloated beach days!

ingredients

dressing

¼ cup (60 ml) extra-virgin olive oil

Juice of 1 lemon

1 teaspoon Dijon mustard

1 garlic clove, smashed

Sea salt or pink salt

Freshly ground black pepper

quinoa salad

1 cup (170 g) dried quinoa

2 cups (330 g) cooked chickpeas (or one 15-ounce/425-g can, rinsed and drained)

1 pint (10 ounces/280 g) cherry tomatoes, sliced lengthwise

1 tablespoon oil of choice

Sea salt or pink salt

5 radishes, thinly sliced

5 scallions, thinly sliced

Freshly ground black pepper

6 large handfuls of arugula

2 avocados, sliced

Lemon wedges

method

Preheat the oven to 375°F (190°C). Line two baking sheets with parchment and set them aside.

For the dressing: Whisk together the olive oil, lemon juice, and mustard. Season to taste with salt and pepper. Add the smashed garlic clove and let it marinate while you continue preparing the salad. Scoop out the garlic clove before pouring it onto the salad.

For the salad: Rinse and drain the quinoa. Put it in a small pot with 2 cups (480 ml) water, stir, and bring it to a boil. Once it's boiling, reduce heat to maintain a simmer, cover, and cook for about 15 minutes. Remove the pot from the heat, fluff the quinoa with a fork, and use a clean kitchen towel or paper towel to cover it. Place the pot lid back on and let the quinoa steam for 5 minutes more, then remove the lid and let it cool completely. The quinoa can be cooked a day in advance.

Spread out the chickpeas on one of the baking sheets and the tomatoes on the other. Using the oil, lightly coat the chickpeas and tomatoes, then sprinkle on a couple generous pinches of salt. Roast until the chickpeas start to turn golden and the tomatoes are glistening and starting to release their juices, about 35 minutes. (Normally I recommend roasting things on the same sheet, but in this case, the tomatoes' juices can make the chickpeas soggy.)

Let the chickpeas and tomatoes cool, then transfer them to a large bowl. Toss them with the quinoa, radishes, scallions, and half of the dressing. Drizzle with additional dressing as needed and season to taste with salt and pepper. Serve over generous handfuls of arugula with slices of avocado and lemon wedges.

berry beet pops

makes 8 to 10 pops

For these pops, the strawberries are blended with coconut water, beets, and coconut butter for the most incredible, refreshing treat. Detox and dessert don't usually go hand in hand, but here beets add a superfood boost, and the creamy coconut butter balances out the natural sugars from the fruit. It's the best of both worlds—a sweet treat and the benefits of a juice all in one.

ingredients

1½ cups (360 ml) young Thai coconut water

1 small beet, peeled and cut into a few pieces

5 strawberries

1 tablespoon coconut butter

method

In a blender, puree all the ingredients until the mixture is completely smooth. Pour it into 3-ounce (90-ml) frozen-pop molds, and freeze for at least 8 hours or overnight.

These will keep a few months in the freezer.

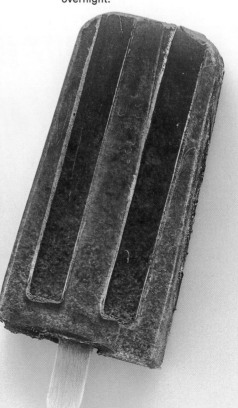

lavender petals

dirty detox bath

magnesium
bath flakes

dirty detox bath

After crossing the street to dodge cigarette smoke and standing in the midst of honking yellow cabs all week, I love to "sweat it out" in a weekly bath. It's a much-needed time of calm and stillness, and helps clear toxins from my system. Detox baths soothe muscles, decrease inflammation, headaches, and anxiety, and improve sleep. I use magnesium bath flakes, which are magically calming, but you can also use Epsom salts as a less expensive option. If doing so, just add a cup of baking soda to the bath.

MAGNESIUM BATH FLAKES
calm, soothe, cleanse, and purify skin.

LAVENDER
is calming and a natural stress reducer.

ROSE PETALS
are relaxing and anti-inflammatory.

ingredients

2 cups (550 g) magnesium bath flakes

1 teaspoon lavender petals (optional)

1 teaspoon dried rose petals (optional)

10 drops lavender oil (optional)

method

Draw a bath with hot water and add the salts, along with the petals and essential oil, if you're using them. Soak for 20 to 30 minutes, rinse off with cool water, and pat dry.

restore

We've all had times when we just need to get better, *stat*. Feeling crappy seems to always come at the most inopportune times—before a big presentation at work, your friend's wedding (even worse, your own), or just when you are about to hop on the plane for vacation. Such a downer.

But wait—the good news is there are lots of foods to support your body (and soul) when you're not feeling your best. No need to overdo it on all those packets of vitamin C from the drugstore, which will likely just get flushed right through your body. Here we turn to real foods that have the good stuff your body knows and loves for healing. These foods are kind of like the chicken soups of our childhood, but packed with even more nutrients. Think ginger, turmeric, citrus, and spices that are antibacterial, immune-boosting, and will kick your body into high gear.

The best thing to do is incorporate all of these foods *before* you start to feel under the weather. If you're feeling great, they will make you feel even better, and if you're just feeling off, they will help bring you back to balance.

sunny immunity bowl

serves 1

Turmeric gets all the credit for this bowl's bright yellow hue, and its taste is reminiscent of a mango lassi—the perfect summer refresher. Coconut milk and the avocado blend into a perfectly creamy, smooth consistency. This bowl is also an antioxidant, anti-inflammatory, and vitamin C powerhouse, thanks to the strawberries, orange, and goji berries. If you'd like to serve it smoothie-style, add more coconut milk, as I've done in my party spread (page 212–213).

ingredients

½ cup (120 ml) coconut milk

¾ cup (120 g) frozen mango

¼ small avocado

½ orange, peeled

Squeeze of lime

1 teaspoon ground turmeric, or 1-inch fresh (start with less if you are not used to the taste)

Few cubes of ice

Top with: sliced strawberries, goji berries, chia seeds, and coconut flakes

method

Pour the coconut milk into a blender; add the mango, avocado, orange, lime juice, turmeric, and ice; puree until smooth.

Pour the smoothie into a bowl and top with strawberries, goji berries, chia seeds, and coconut flakes.

immune-boosting shot

makes 1 double shot

Natural remedy fanatics *all* agree that some version of this shot is mandatory. It's a super-concentrated shot of anti-inflammatory, antibacterial, and antimicrobial ingredients that combine to boost immunity. And the strong taste is not for the faint of heart. If you are feeling brave, my secret to avoiding colds is adding a clove of raw garlic (you can grate it in), or simply swallowing a clove whole. Garlic is filled with antibiotic and antifungal compounds—anything to get rid of that cough, right? The pinch of cayenne is optional, but it can help clear congestion and remove toxins from the body. Bottoms up!

ingredients

Juice of 1 lemon

½ teaspoon grated, peeled fresh ginger

½ teaspoon grated, peeled fresh turmeric

2 drops oil of oregano

Pinch of freshly ground black pepper

Pinch of cayenne (optional)

1 garlic clove, grated (optional)

method

Mix all the ingredients together in a small glass (or double shot glass). Alternatively, double the batch and blend it up in a mini food processor or blender.

turn up for TURMERIC

Turmeric is magically healing and a powerful anti-inflammatory that can be helpful for a number of health issues—arthritis, digestion, a weak immune system, skin issues, brain function, and cancer. And it's all because it contains the very powerful antioxidant curcumin, which gives turmeric its bright orange color. Curcumin is not very bioavailable (easily absorbed) on its own, but there are two things you can do to get its benefits. One option is to add a dash of freshly ground black pepper to any dish you use turmeric in; this increases the bioavailability by 2,000 percent. Or enjoy it with a healthy fat, like avocado, as in the sunny immunity bowl (page 130).

You can purchase turmeric fresh or in dried form, similar to how you find ginger. I prefer to use fresh turmeric in smoothies, immunity shots, and teas, whereas the dried turmeric is great for curries, soups, and roasted vegetables. It also works well in smoothies—in fact, a 1-inch (2.5-cm) piece of fresh turmeric is pretty interchangeable for 1 teaspoon of dried turmeric.

the daily bowl

serves 2

This bowl borrows its concept from the macroplate—a perfectly balanced serving of rice, beans, steamed vegetables, steamed greens, and sea vegetables in traditional macrobiotic cuisine. I call it the daily bowl because there is always a different grain or bean du jour in my kitchen; it's also my go-to when I need to get back to balance. Here it's served with black rice, mung beans, and fermented sauerkraut, but you can customize it to your liking. Sea veggies are rich in minerals and chlorophyll, which balance pH and detoxify the body. Hijiki and sea palm are two of my favorites.

ingredients

1 cup (195 g) cooked black rice

1 cup (124 g) cooked mung beans (or one 15-ounce/425-g can white beans)

1 small sweet potato, cubed and steamed

2 cups (180 g) broccoli florets, steamed

1 bunch curly or Tuscan kale, stems removed, roughly chopped and steamed

½ avocado, thinly sliced

Top with: raw fermented sauerkraut, sea vegetables, microgreens, sprouts, hemp hearts, gomasio (page 38)

Miso-tahini dressing (recipe follows)

Green tahini dressing (page 161)

Miso-ginger dressing (page 34)

method

Assemble the bowls by spooning in generous portions of rice, beans, sweet potato, broccoli, kale, and avocado. Add your choice of toppings and drizzle on one or more of the dressings.

miso-tahini dressing

makes 1 cup (240 ml)

ingredients

½ cup (120 ml) tahini

2 tablespoons miso

Juice of 1 lemon

Freshly ground black pepper

method

Combine the tahini, miso, and lemon juice, along with pepper to taste, in a small bowl. While whisking, gradually add up to ½ cup (120 ml) water until you reach your desired consistency.

curry-cauli bowl

serves 2 generously

Cauliflower is among the most humble of vegetables, but here transforms into a caramelized, crispy veggie that can hold its own as the star of the party. If you're looking for a heartier dish, toss in some cooked chickpeas with the cauliflower before roasting. Just add a splash more oil and an additional pinch of salt. While I love the combination of quinoa, millet, and buckwheat, the bowl is just as good made with only quinoa.

ingredients

1 small head cauliflower, cut into small florets

2 shallots, thinly sliced

2 tablespoons coconut oil, melted

1 teaspoon curry powder

½ teaspoon ground turmeric

Sea salt or pink salt

Freshly ground black pepper

Pinch of red pepper flakes (optional)

1 cup (175 g) mixed quinoa, millet, and buckwheat

¼ cup (25 g) sliced almonds, toasted

¼ cup (10 g) roughly chopped cilantro

Juice of ½ lime, plus more as needed

Olive oil

2 handfuls of greens such as arugula, or chopped spinach

CFDC vinaigrette (page 34)

method

Preheat the oven to 400°F (205°C) and line a baking sheet with parchment. Toss the cauliflower florets with the shallots, coconut oil, curry powder, turmeric, and a couple of pinches of salt and pepper. If you'd like, add a pinch of red pepper flakes for some heat. Roast the cauliflower for 35 to 40 minutes, or until the florets are cooked through and golden.

Meanwhile, rinse the grains and add them to a pot with 2 cups (480 ml) water. Give it a nice stir, add a pinch of salt, and bring it to a boil. Cover and reduce the heat to maintain a simmer for 15 to 18 minutes. Remove the pot from the heat, place a paper towel or kitchen towel on top of the pot, replace the lid, and let the grains steam for 5 to 10 minutes. Remove the lid, fluff the grains, and let them cool to room temperature. Stir in the toasted almonds, cilantro, lime, a drizzle of olive oil, and salt and pepper to taste.

Serve a generous portion of the grains in each bowl, topped with the cauliflower and greens. Drizzle with the CFDC vinaigrette and more olive oil or lime as desired.

red lentil earth curry

serves 4 to 6

ingredients

1 tablespoon coconut oil or ghee

1 onion, diced

2 carrots, diced

5 garlic cloves, minced

2-inch (5-cm) piece fresh ginger, peeled and minced

2 cups (230 g) bite-size cubes winter squash (see Note)

1 cup (200 g) red lentils

1 tablespoon curry powder

Pinch of red pepper flakes (optional)

1 cup (240 ml) coconut milk

3 to 4 cups (720 to 960 ml) vegetable broth

2 tablespoons low-sodium gluten-free tamari

2 handfuls of chopped spinach (or Tuscan kale)

2 handfuls of cilantro, chopped, plus more for garnish

Pinch of coconut sugar

Squeeze of lime

Sea salt or pink salt

Freshly ground black pepper

When I eat out, I love going for dishes that are gluten-free without modification. That's why curry is a favorite at Thai or Indian restaurants—it is always bursting with bold, vibrant flavors. Now I've found a simple way to make this restorative dish at home. The onions and chili are powerful anti-inflammatories and antihistamines, and the garlic is an antibacterial. It's everything you would want in a bowl when you aren't feeling 100 percent. If you want more heat, add red pepper flakes or fresh chiles.

method

In a large heavy-bottomed pot, heat the oil over medium-high. Add the onion and carrots and sauté for 5 to 7 minutes. Add the garlic and ginger and sauté for 1 minute more until fragrant. Add the squash, lentils, curry powder, and red pepper flakes (if you're using them). Cook for 1 to 2 minutes, stirring frequently and being careful not to burn the spices.

Add the coconut milk, 3 cups (720 ml) of the vegetable broth, and the tamari. Bring the mixture to a simmer and cook for 25 to 30 minutes until the squash and lentils are soft. If you would like a thinner curry, add more broth, otherwise leave as is.

Remove the pan from the burner and immediately stir in the spinach and cilantro (they will wilt from the heat). Add a pinch of coconut sugar, if you like, and a squeeze of lime, and season to taste with salt and black pepper.

Ladle the curry into bowls. Garnish it with additional cilantro, lime, and fresh red pepper if you like. Enjoy!

note:
Kabocha squash has the creamiest, sweetest flesh. It is available at most well-stocked grocers or farmers' markets in the winter, so use one in this dish if you can; otherwise, butternut squash is a good substitute.

miso mushroom soup

serves 2

ingredients

1 tablespoon coconut oil

1 large leek, sliced

2 carrots, chopped

1 teaspoon peeled, minced fresh ginger

1 garlic clove, minced

4-inch (10-cm) piece kombu

4 ounces (115 g) shiitake mushrooms, sliced

1 daikon radish or zucchini, spiralized

3 tablespoons chickpea miso, plus more to taste

2 Tuscan kale leaves, stems removed, thinly sliced (optional)

Scallions, for garnish

Miso soup is my chicken soup. Miso is a paste most commonly made from fermented soybeans, and through the fermentation process, miso becomes a close friend to the digestive system by promoting healthy bacteria in the gut. This version is made a bit heartier with mushrooms and spiralized noodles. I especially love the daikon radish here—it's very mild once cooked and is beneficial for both detoxification and boosting the immune system. Be sure to ladle some broth into the miso and whisk well before adding it to the pot to avoid clumps of miso in the soup (you're going for velvety perfection!).

method

Heat the coconut oil in a medium pot until it shimmers. Add the leek and carrots and cook for 2 minutes. Add the ginger and garlic and sauté for an additional 2 minutes. Add 5 cups (1.2 L) water, the kombu, and mushrooms, and bring the mixture to a boil. Reduce the heat and simmer the broth, covered, for about 15 minutes. Add the spiralized daikon radish and simmer for 5 minutes longer. Remove the kombu.

In a small bowl, ladle 1 cup (240 ml) of the broth from the pot and whisk in the miso. Gently pour the broth back into the pot, add the kale, and stir until it is just wilted. Taste and season with additional miso as needed.

Divide the daikon noodles into two bowls and ladle the broth over them. Garnish with scallions.

tip:
Add some rehydrated wakame for an extra mineral-rich boost.

notes:
Misos vary in how salty they are. If you are using a white miso instead of a chickpea miso, start with 2 tablespoons and add more to taste.

If you have some dashi on hand (page 55), you can substitute it for the 5 cups (1.2 L) water, the kombu, and mushrooms.

make room for MUSHROOMS

Mushrooms are incredible immune-boosters! Even the most humble of mushrooms are sources of antioxidants and have anti-inflammatory, antiviral, and antibacterial properties. They can also help regulate cholesterol and blood pressure. While your standard mushroom (think white or cremini) is healthy, mushrooms like shiitake and reishi reign as queen, with super levels of healing powers.

Mushrooms can also be purchased dried, and they have an intense, umami quality that adds flavor to soups and stocks. When cooked, mushrooms acquire a satisfying, meaty texture, making them the perfect option for a hearty meal like my spaghetti with mushroom meatballs (page 90). Another easy option for these cancer and flu fighters is to sauté them with some ghee and fresh thyme and serve alongside wild rice and greens.

gingery carrot soup + smashed avo-toast

serves 4

Carrot ginger soup is a classic combo that I rely on when I get the first hint of a sore throat. It's warm and soothing, but most importantly, it's easy. Packed full of ginger and turmeric—both powerful anti-inflammatories—and coconut oil, an antibacterial, this minimalist, basically five-ingredient soup is powerful. Be sure to puree the soup; it means less work for your digestive system, which allows the nutrients to be easily accessed and equals a quicker recovery for you. Don't forget to serve it with avocado toast; we all know that makes everything better.

ingredients

carrot soup

1 tablespoon coconut oil or ghee

1 medium onion, chopped

2 tablespoons peeled, minced fresh ginger

1 garlic clove, minced

1 teaspoon ground turmeric

2 pounds (910 g) carrots, chopped

4 to 5 cups (960 ml to 1.2 L) basic veggie broth (page 50) or vegan bone broth (page 52), or low-sodium vegetable stock

Sea salt or pink salt

Freshly ground black pepper

¼ cup (15 g) toasted pepitas

avocado toast

4 slices gluten-free bread

1 ripe avocado

Juice of ½ lemon

Drizzle of olive oil

Pinch of red pepper flakes

Pinch of Maldon salt

method

For the soup: Heat the oil in a large heavy-bottomed pot over medium. When it shimmers, add the onion and sauté until softened, 5 to 7 minutes. Add the ginger and garlic and sauté for 2 minutes. Add the turmeric and carrots and sauté for another minute, then add 4 cups (960 ml) of the broth and simmer for 20 to 25 minutes, until carrots are tender.

Remove the pot from the heat, and let it cool slightly. Use an immersion blender or transfer the soup to a blender and blend until it is nearly smooth but with some texture from the carrots. Alternatively, blend until velvety smooth if that is your preference. If needed, add more broth or water to thin it to the desired consistency. Season with salt and pepper to taste.

For the avocado toast: Toast the bread. Mash ¼ avocado directly on each piece of bread. Drizzle each slice with the lemon juice, olive oil, and a pinch each of red pepper flakes and flaky salt.

Ladle the soup into bowls and top it with the pepitas. Serve the avocado toast alongside.

all greens soup

serves 4

ingredients

1 tablespoon
coconut oil or ghee

1 large leek, cleaned
and thinly sliced

1 large carrot,
chopped

Sea salt or pink salt

2 garlic cloves,
minced

2 zucchini, chopped

1 head of broccoli,
cut into florets

3 to 4 cups (720 to
960 ml) basic veggie
broth (page 50) or
vegan bone broth
(page 52)

2 large handfuls
of spinach

⅓ cup (75 ml)
cashew milk
(page 48)

Freshly ground
black pepper

Serve with:
microgreens or
sprouts

This is my "winter green juice." Like juice, it is packed with greens and easy on your digestive system, but it's also full of fiber, warming, and rich with alkalinizing minerals and detoxifying greens. It's reminiscent of a cream of broccoli soup, but finds its creaminess instead from the zucchini and rich cashew milk. Feel free to experiment with other veggies, like kale, chard, or cauliflower. Kale and chard add a slightly bitter flavor, whereas a few pieces of cauliflower result in an even creamier soup. With any combination, this is perfect for a cold day—sip on it to warm up and instantly boost your energy and spirit.

method

Heat a medium Dutch oven over medium-high and add the oil. When it shimmers, add the leek, carrot, and a pinch of salt, and sauté for 7 to 10 minutes, until softened. Add the garlic and sauté for 1 minute. Add the zucchini and broccoli, and pour in enough broth to just cover the veggies. Bring the soup to a boil, reduce the heat, and simmer until the veggies are just cooked through, 7 to 10 minutes.

Remove the pot from the heat and let it cool slightly. Add the spinach, and using an immersion blender, puree the soup until it is velvety smooth. (You can also use a regular blender and puree in batches.) Stir in the cashew milk and season with salt and pepper to taste.

Serve the soup topped with microgreens or sprouts.

manuka honey +
tea tree oil

healing honey
face mask

lemon

fresh turmeric

healing honey face mask

makes 1 mask

This has been my go-to face mask for years—I use it when my skin is dry, broken out, and for everything else in between. It's also perfect for when you are feeling puffy or tired. Combining manuka honey with lemon, tea tree oil, and turmeric, this face mask fights bacteria and leaves you with a soft glow.

MANUKA HONEY
is healing, antimicrobial, and gently exfoliating to the skin.

LEMONS
are antibacterial and rich in vitamin C, which can help lighten dark spots and even out skin tone.

TEA TREE OIL
is an antiseptic that fights bacteria, viruses, and fungi.

TURMERIC
is anti-inflammatory and rich in antioxidants, which help fight free-radical damage.

ingredients

½ tablespoon manuka honey or raw honey

Squeeze of lemon

2 drops of tea tree oil

Dash of ground turmeric or grated fresh turmeric

method

In a medium bowl, combine all the ingredients and mix well. Spread a thin layer over your face. Leave it on for 10 to 30 minutes, then rinse well and moisturize immediately.

magic MANUKA

Manuka honey is a specific type of honey from the manuka bush in New Zealand and Australia. It has a number of health benefits: Just a spoonful of manuka honey may help your sore throat go away—it's highly antimicrobial, filled with minerals and antioxidants. If you're looking for medicinal manuka honey, look for one with a Unique Manuka Factor (UMF) of at least 10. These honeys are guaranteed to contain a natural hydrogen peroxide that works as an antibacterial. If you can't get your hands on manuka, look for local, raw honey, which has similar properties.

Genuine manuka honey is very stable, making it perfect to be stirred into hot teas and drinks or simply taken as a small spoonful each day. While it's delicious, my favorite way to use manuka honey is for beauty treatments. It has natural exfoliating and healing properties that instantly soothe and reveal baby-soft skin.

sustain

even if you have breakfast down—it gives you tons of energy and fuel for a productive morning—for some reason, the afternoon slump seems to *always* roll in, no matter what you do. And to make matters worse, this is the time when the candy bars and bags of chips really start screaming your name. You might give in, but you probably won't feel any better. We're not trying to crash and burn here.

You need foods that are satisfying, filling, and energizing to get you through any time of the day (but especially the afternoon slump). Healthy fats like avocados and nuts, whole grains, and beans are a sugar-balancing, effective way to keep you full and help avoid the crash. The more you incorporate these balanced foods into your diet, the more your cravings will start to reduce.

The recipes in this chapter are ideal for those days when you know you'll have a late dinner, or when there's a long travel day ahead of you, or really any day you need an extra-special snack. If you munch on this food throughout the day, you won't crash later. Also, who can ever say no to sweet potato fries?!

mint-chip shake

makes 2 servings

Mint chocolate chip ice cream was my all-time favorite as a kid, largely because of the neon green color. My preferences have shifted since then, but I'm still all for a beautiful, bright green shade if it's made from spirulina, chlorella, or spinach! In this smoothie, the peppermint mimics the classic ice cream flavor. Combined with creamy avocado, crunchy cacao nibs, and some natural sweetness from the raw honey, this makes an out-of-this-world midday energy bump. Use stevia in place of the raw honey, if you prefer.

ingredients

1 cup (240 ml) cashew or brazil nut milk, or any plant-based milk (page 48)

½ small avocado

2 handfuls of spinach

1 teaspoon super greens powder (I like Philosophie Green Dream)

¼ cup (13 g) fresh mint leaves, packed

2 to 3 teaspoons raw honey, or a few drops of stevia

Dash of pure vanilla extract

Pinch of sea salt or pink salt

Few cubes of ice

Organic peppermint oil or peppermint extract

1 tablespoon cacao nibs, plus more for topping

method

In a blender, combine the nut milk, avocado, spinach, green powder, mint leaves, 2 teaspoons of the honey, the vanilla, salt, and ice. Add a few drops of peppermint oil—if you're using the extract, you'll need more than that. Puree until the mixture is well combined. Taste and adjust the honey as needed.

Blend again, then add the cacao nibs and pulse briefly to combine.

Serve the shake topped with additional cacao nibs, if desired.

back that HASS up

I have an addiction to all kinds of avocados. There are hundreds of varieties, from the Hass to two of my favorites, the Fuerte and the Bacon. Avocados have a high fat content—but the *good* kind of fat—making them not only anti-inflammatory but also useful for regulating blood pressure and blood sugar. They're also a heart-healthy food because of their high level of monounsaturated fats, which can help lower bad cholesterol and raise good cholesterol.

Eaten alone, avocados are nutrient-dense, but their benefits continue even when you're eating other foods. They help you absorb fat-soluble nutrients like lycopene and beta-carotene in vegetables such as tomatoes and carrots that are essential for heart health. This is the best excuse to eat avocado toast with just about everything, like tomato soup or gingery carrot soup (page 144). Or add avocado to salads and veggie bowls!

citrus coconut oats

Citrus fruits are like pockets of sunshine in the winter, reminding us that warmer days are ahead. In this bowl, I love the layers of bright citrus paired with the creaminess of the coconut milk and crunch of toasted coconut flakes. The oats are soaked in coconut milk and fresh-squeezed orange juice, which adds a natural sweetness, and then topped with an orange chia jam for another layer of subtle sweetness. Enjoy with your favorite citrus medley.

ingredients

soaked oats

2 cups (180 g) gluten-free rolled oats

1½ cups (360 ml) coconut milk

¼ cup (60 ml) fresh orange juice

1 teaspoon orange zest

Dash of pure vanilla extract

Dash of ground cardamom

Dash of ground ginger

Dash of ground cinnamon

1 to 2 teaspoons raw honey (optional)

orange chia jam

1 tablespoon white chia seeds

¼ cup (60 ml) fresh orange juice

toppings

Assorted citrus slices: Pomelo orange, blood orange, or grapefruit

Toasted coconut flakes

Bee pollen

method

For the oats: In a large jar or glass container, combine the oats, milk, juice, zest, vanilla, and spices. Let them soak in the refrigerator overnight. Give the mixture a good stir in the morning. Taste and add the raw honey, if desired. Store the oats in the fridge for up to 3 days.

For the jam: In a small jar, combine the chia seeds and the orange juice. Stir well, place the mixture in the fridge, and let it sit for at least 30 minutes, or up to overnight. Give it a good stir before serving. It will keep in the fridge for 3 to 5 days.

To assemble: Put a big scoop of the soaked oats in a small jar or a bowl and top it with the chia jam, citrus slices or supremes (see Note), toasted coconut flakes, and bee pollen.

note:
Cutting your citrus into "supremes" is not as hard as it looks! Start by trimming the top and bottom of your fruit with a sharp knife. Then cut the skin away from the flesh, starting at the top of the fruit and curving down to the bottom. Once the skin is removed, you will be left with just the flesh and the membrane between the segments. Carefully remove each section by cutting on both sides between the citrus flesh and the membrane. The wedges should easily slide out. Repeat until each wedge has been removed!

lazy lentil salad

serves 4 to 6

I make this simple salad on Sundays, and it's labeled as *lazy* in the most endearing way possible. It takes almost zero effort to put together and is delicious served with whole grains and roasted vegetables. Lentils are a good source of protein and are full of fiber, which stabilizes blood sugar and sustains your energy for hours. They're a hearty, but not heavy, addition to any meal. The beautiful brightness from the fresh herbs and lemon enhance the salad. It's a crowd-pleaser.

ingredients

1 cup (200 g) black lentils or French green lentils

1-inch (2.5-cm) piece kombu

½ onion

2 garlic cloves, crushed

¼ cup (60 ml) olive oil

Juice of 1 to 2 lemons

½ shallot, finely minced

¼ teaspoon Dijon mustard

Sea salt or pink salt

Freshly ground black pepper

¼ cup (13 g) roughly chopped parsley

2 tablespoons chives, thinly sliced

Microgreens (optional)

method

Rinse and drain the lentils. In a medium pot, add the lentils, kombu, onion, and garlic, and cover with at least 2 inches (5 cm) of cold water. Bring the water to a boil, reduce the heat, and simmer for 15 to 20 minutes. When the lentils are nearly cooked through, add ½ teaspoon salt and cook for the remaining time. Taste the lentils as they simmer—you want them to be firm but cooked through. When they're done, remove the kombu, onion, and garlic. Drain and rinse the lentils with cool water.

In a small bowl, whisk together the olive oil, the juice from one of the lemons, the shallot, mustard, 1 teaspoon salt, and pepper to taste. Set aside.

Transfer the lentils to a large bowl and gently fold in the dressing with the parsley and chives. Season the dish with additional salt, pepper, and lemon to taste. Top with microgreens, if desired.

Enjoy the lentils alone or serve them over your favorite greens and with whole grains.

---

love for LENTILS

Lentils come in many different varieties, shapes, and sizes—there's a lot to love! They are full of complex carbohydrates and fiber, which balance blood sugar, increase energy, aid digestion, and keep you full. They are also beneficial for heart health and can help lower cholesterol.

There's no need to pick just one type of lentil—my legume of choice completely depends on the occasion. French lentils (or "du Puy") and black lentils are both great for salads because they hold their shape when cooked. Other lentils, like green, brown, and, especially, red are better in soups and stews—they break down and add a nice texture as in my red lentil earth curry (page 140). Legumes are easy on the wallet and easy to find—you can pick them up at well-stocked grocery stores or in the bulk section of natural grocers.

moroccan chickpea + carrot salad

serves 4 to 6

ingredients

1 bunch of rainbow carrots, washed and trimmed

1 small red onion, cut into ½-inch (12-mm) pieces

2 cups (330 g) cooked chickpeas (or one 15-ounce/423-g can, rinsed and drained)

2 tablespoons coconut oil

1 teaspoon ground cumin

½ teaspoon ground cinnamon

½ teaspoon garlic powder

¼ teaspoon ground turmeric

Dash of cayenne

Sea salt or pink salt

Freshly ground black pepper

Drizzle of olive oil

Juice of ½ lemon, plus more for serving

¼ cup (30 g) sliced almonds, toasted

¼ cup (8 g) parsley, roughly chopped

Throw this together for a flavorful, easy lunch. It travels extremely well. Roasting the chickpeas and carrots helps them get all crispy and caramelized, and above all delicious. Don't forget the toasted almonds for that extra crunch.

method

Preheat the oven to 425°F (220°C). Line a rimmed baking sheet with parchment and set aside. Cut the carrots into ¼-inch (6-mm) rounds; place on the baking sheet along with the onion, chickpeas, and coconut oil. Toss well and add the spices, salt, and pepper.

Roast for 25 to 35 minutes, tossing halfway, until caramelized and cooked through. Remove from the oven and toss with a drizzle of olive oil and squeeze of lemon. Season with salt and pepper to taste and add more olive oil and lemon as needed.

Stir in the toasted almonds and parsley, and enjoy alone or over greens with an additional squeeze of lemon.

mediterranean falafel bowl with green tahini dressing

makes 20 falafel; serves 4

Falafel is a favorite indulgence of mine. This baked—instead of fried—version delivers the familiar, delicious flavors in a much healthier, always gluten-free way. I pair it with millet salad rather than your traditional tabbouleh, which uses bulgur wheat. Millet is one of the most alkalinizing and easiest grains to digest.

ingredients

mediterranean grain salad

1 cup (200 g) millet

Sea salt or pink salt

1 English cucumber, unpeeled, seeded, and cut into medium dice

1 pint (10 ounces/280 g) cherry tomatoes, halved

½ cup (25 g) chopped parsley

Juice of 1 lemon

⅓ cup (90 ml) olive oil

Freshly ground black pepper

herbed falafel

⅓ cup (50 g) walnuts (or almonds)

2 cups (330 g) cooked chickpeas (or one 15-ounce/425-g can, rinsed and drained)

½ yellow onion, chopped

2 garlic cloves, minced

2 tablespoons olive oil, plus more for brushing

1 tablespoon tahini

Juice of 1 lemon

1 tablespoon buckwheat, chickpea, or other gluten-free flour

1 teaspoon baking soda

1 teaspoon ground cumin

1 teaspoon salt

¼ cup (8 g) mixed herbs (such as parsley, mint, cilantro, and chives)

Freshly ground black pepper to taste

green tahini dressing

½ cup (120 ml) tahini

½ cup (16 g) parsley

Juice of 2 lemons

2 garlic cloves

Sea salt or pink salt

Freshly ground black pepper

Serve with: mixed greens or arugula and hemp hearts

method

Preheat the oven to 375°F (190°C). Line a baking sheet with parchment and set aside.

For the salad: In a large pan, toast the millet over medium heat for 3 to 4 minutes, or until the grains start to turn golden brown. Meanwhile, in a small pot, bring 2 cups (480 ml) water to a boil. Add the millet and a pinch of salt, stir, cover, reduce the heat, and simmer for 15 to 20 minutes. Remove the pot from the heat and cover it with a kitchen towel to let the millet steam for 5 to 10 minutes. Gently fluff the grains and let them cool to room temperature.

Meanwhile, combine the cucumbers, tomatoes, parsley, lemon juice, olive oil, and salt and pepper to taste in a large bowl. Once the millet is nearly cool, add to the bowl and stir well. Season with salt and pepper to taste.

For the falafel: In a food processor, pulse the walnuts until they are fine and crumbly. Add the chickpeas, onion, and garlic, and pulse a few more times. Add the remaining ingredients and pulse until a nice texture is achieved and the ingredients are well combined. Use a tablespoon-size cookie scoop or a tablespoon to scoop out the mixture. Moisten your hands with water or oil and gently roll the mix into balls and place them on the parchment. Repeat with the remaining mixture. Use a pastry brush to brush the tops of the falafel with oil. Bake for about 25 minutes, or until the falafel is golden on all sides, flipping them halfway through.

For the dressing: In a food processor or blender, blend the tahini, parsley, lemon juice, and garlic until well combined. Slowly drizzle in water as needed until you reach a pourable consistency. Season with salt and pepper to taste. Store in an airtight container in the fridge for up to 4 days.

Serve the falafel in a bowl with the millet salad, greens, hemp hearts, and a generous drizzle of the green tahini dressing.

sweet potato fries
with cashew ranch dip

serves 2 to 4

sweet potato fries

2 small to medium sweet potatoes, cut into ¼-inch (6-mm) matchsticks

2 teaspoons melted coconut oil or oil of choice

2 teaspoons mixed spices such as chili powder, garlic powder, and ground turmeric

Pinch of cayenne

Sea salt or pink salt

Freshly ground black pepper

This recipe might be my hands-down favorite snack ever. Sweet, crispy on the outside, and slightly spicy, these fries disappear once they hit the plate. Unlike regular French fries, sweet potato fries are much more nutrient-dense, and won't slow you down. The key to getting them to crisp up is giving them enough room to breathe on the pan—they shouldn't touch each other!—so they don't end up steaming. Serve with creamy cashew ranch dip.

cashew ranch dip

1 cup (120 g) raw cashews, soaked overnight and drained

½ cup (120 ml) water or unsweetened almond milk (page 48)

Juice of 1 to 2 lemons

1 teaspoon garlic powder

1 teaspoon onion powder

Dash of cayenne

Dash of paprika

½ teaspoon sea salt or pink salt

¼ cup (8 g) minced mixed chives, dill, and parsley

Freshly ground black pepper

method

For the fries: Preheat the oven to 400°F (205°C). Line a rimmed baking sheet with parchment and set aside. Lightly coat the sweet potatoes with the oil and toss them with the spices and a few pinches of salt and pepper.

Lay the potatoes out on the baking sheet in a single layer. Make sure they don't touch, as this will help them crisp up. Bake them for 35 to 40 minutes, turning them halfway through. They are done when they are golden on both sides and cooked through. Let them cool slightly before serving.

For the dip: In a food processor or blender, combine the cashews, water, juice of one of the lemons, garlic and onion powders, cayenne, paprika, and salt. Puree until the mixture is creamy. If needed, add more water to reach your desired consistency. Transfer the dip to a small bowl, stir in the herbs, and season with additional lemon juice and salt and pepper to taste. Chill for 30 minutes before serving to let the flavors meld.

zucchini almond dip

makes about 1½ cups (360 ml)

As much as I love hummus, it's nice to change it up with some unexpected dips like this one. Zucchini lends such a creamy texture to dips, soups, and even smoothies. Here I've paired the zucchini with soaked almonds—this added protein will keep you full. If you serve with lavash, look for one that's gluten-free. The one I buy is made from millet, brown rice, and ground flaxseed, making it a high-fiber pairing for your dip.

ingredients

½ cup (70 g) raw almonds

Sea salt or pink salt

1 small zucchini, roughly chopped

Juice of 1 lemon

¼ cup (60 ml) olive oil

1 garlic clove, minced

¼ teaspoon ground cumin

Serve with: toasted gluten-free lavash (see Note) or flax crackers, olives, and vegetables

method

In a large bowl, cover the almonds with water and a few pinches of salt. Soak them overnight in the fridge, or at least 8 to 12 hours.

Rinse and drain the almonds. In a food processor, combine the almonds, zucchini, lemon juice, 1 tablespoon of the olive oil, the garlic, cumin, and ¼ teaspoon salt, and pulse. Continue adding the olive oil, 1 tablespoon at a time, and blend until the dip is creamy but not completely smooth. Adjust salt to taste (I usually add a few more pinches) and pulse until it is incorporated. The dip will keep in a jar in the fridge for up to 4 days.

Serve it with toasted lavash, flax crackers, olives, and vegetables.

note:
To toast the lavash, preheat the oven to 350°F (175°C). Brush the lavash with a thin layer of oil and a few pinches of flaky salt, cut it into chips, and toast for 10 minutes, or until it starts to turn golden. Let the crisps cool and serve them with the dip. Toasting time will vary slightly depending on your lavash, so watch carefully the first time!

mango macarons

makes about 10 macarons

This version of a macaron turns the decadent dessert into a quick snack, ditching the refined sugar and replacing it with sweet mango and raw honey. Cashews and coconut flakes are both healthy fats (your brain needs these fats to function properly!), while the honey adds just the touch of sweetness you crave in the afternoon. These are designed to keep you full—like the walnut orange globes on page 72—and make an easy travel snack or a healthy pre- or post-workout treat.

ingredients

½ cup (60 g) raw cashews

½ cup (45 g) coconut flakes, plus 2 tablespoons for rolling

½ cup (50 g) chopped dried mango

1 teaspoon raw honey

½ teaspoon pure vanilla extract

Sea salt or pink salt

Splash of plant-based milk (page 48), as needed

method

In a food processor, combine the cashews and coconut flakes and process until you have a crumbly mixture. Add the mango, honey, vanilla, and a pinch of salt, and pulse until well combined. The mixture should stick together when pinched. Add a splash of plant-based milk if needed.

Roll the mixture into balls using a small cookie scoop (or about 2 teaspoons of dough), and roll them in the coconut flakes to coat. Place the balls on a parchment-lined plate and chill them for 30 minutes before serving. Store in an airtight container in the fridge for up to a week or in the freezer for 3 months.

mini carrot gingerbread muffins with chai cashew cream

makes 24 mini muffins

My aunt Carol is a chef and one of my biggest inspirations in the kitchen. It's been so fun sharing the same passion, especially when we create a recipe like this one. Gluten-free and vegan muffins can be tough to master—you can end up with muffins that either fell flat or that are rather dense. But you won't find that here! The recipe is so simple. You use only one flour, and the result is a perfectly spiced, fluffy gingerbread with a moist, cakelike texture from the carrots. Don't let the leftover chai cashew cream go to waste! Try it on chia puddings, or even as an extra-special treat on top of oatmeal, pancakes, or waffles.

ingredients

chai cashew cream

½ cup (60 g) raw cashews

Raw apple cider vinegar

1½ tablespoons coconut sugar

½ teaspoon pure vanilla extract

½ teaspoon ground cinnamon

½ teaspoon grated, peeled fresh ginger

¼ teaspoon ground cardamom

carrot gingerbread muffins

1¼ cups (150 g) buckwheat flour

1 tablespoon pumpkin-pie spice

½ teaspoon baking powder

1 teaspoon baking soda

¼ teaspoon sea salt or pink salt

2 teaspoons finely grated, peeled fresh ginger

1½ cups (165 g) finely grated carrot

1 cup (190 g) coconut sugar

2 pasture-raised eggs or flax eggs (see Note, page 82)

⅓ cup (75 ml) coconut oil, melted

Hemp hearts, for sprinkling

method

For the cashew cream: Rinse the cashews and soak them for 8 hours or overnight, covered with water and a splash of apple cider vinegar. Rinse them well and, using an immersion blender or mini food processor, blend the cashews, sugar, vanilla, cinnamon, ginger, cardamom, and 6 tablespoons (90 ml) water together until you have a smooth paste. You can also use a regular blender, but you will need to double the frosting recipe.

For the muffins: Preheat the oven to 350°F (175°C) and prepare a mini muffin tin with paper liners. In a large bowl, combine the flour, spice, baking powder, baking soda, and salt. Whisk well to remove any lumps and thoroughly combine.

In a separate bowl, combine the ginger, carrot, coconut sugar, and eggs, and whisk until just mixed. Then whisk in the coconut oil until combined. Add the wet ingredients to the dry and mix well.

Scoop the batter into the mini muffin cups, filling them to the top. Bake for 14 minutes, or until a toothpick inserted into a muffin comes out clean. Let them cool completely before proceeding.

Frost the muffins just before serving. Use a small spoon to dollop cashew cream on top of each one and sprinkle it with hemp hearts. Store leftover frosting in the fridge for up to 4 days.

midday matcha latte

serves 2

I wasn't planning to include this recipe until it became a daily occurrence on set while shooting the book! When afternoon rolled around, I always blended up a big batch of matchas for the crew. This is the modern version of the matcha—I didn't have a whisk on me, but the result is just as delicious. It gave us all the energy to finish fun but long days on set with a calm and energized focus. I love it with homemade cashew milk, but feel free to substitute any milk of your choice.

ingredients

2 cups (480 ml) cashew milk (page 48)

2 teaspoons ceremonial grade matcha powder

1 teaspoon raw honey (optional)

method

In a small pot over medium-low, gently warm the cashew milk for about 5 minutes. Be careful not to boil it.

Transfer the milk to a blender and blend it with the matcha and honey, if you're using it, until frothy, about 1 minute. Pour into mugs—cheers!

manuka honey

matcha powder

brightening green
tea face mask

cucumber

parsley

brightening green tea face mask

makes 2 masks

Matcha doesn't only wake you up via a creamy latte. It's also just as effective when applied on the outside. This face mask awakens your skin, revealing a brighter, more rejuvenated appearance. Combined with the cucumber, this concoction is perfect for a puffy or tired face. You'll have enough for two masks, so if you don't have a friend around, store it in the fridge for a double treatment two nights in a row.

Tip: Draw a warm bath and relax with your mask on. The heat will help activate the hydrogen peroxide in the honey, which gives it its antibiotic quality and makes it more effective and potent.

CUCUMBER
is deeply hydrating, while reducing swelling and puffiness.

MATCHA POWDER
is high in antioxidants, which fight free radicals and help repair damaged skin.

PARSLEY
is antibacterial and rich in vitamins and minerals that boost collagen production and reduce inflammation.

MANUKA HONEY
is a powerful antibacterial that gently exfoliates and cleanses while deeply nourishing the skin at the same time.

ingredients

1-inch (2.5-cm) piece cucumber, finely grated

1 tablespoon finely minced parsley

½ teaspoon matcha powder

1 to 2 drops tea tree oil (optional, for oily skin)

1 tablespoon manuka honey or raw honey

method

In a small bowl, mix the cucumber, parsley, and matcha powder to make a creamy paste. Make sure the parsley is minced well—after mincing it, you can even smash it in a mortar and pestle to create more of a paste. Add tea tree oil, if you're using it, and the honey, and stir. Apply the mask to your face and leave it on for 15 to 20 minutes. To remove it, rinse well with cool water.

savor

The sugar rushes of my childhood came in the form of bonbons at my grandma's, strawberry shortcake Popsicles by the pool, and apple pie on Thanksgiving. We had a cookie jar filled with homemade chocolate chip cookies on the counter, and there was always another batch baking in the oven. Friends were never disappointed when they came over. And you know what? It's totally fine to savor these things— it's about finding balance so that you *can* eat healthily most of the time instead of depriving yourself and then promptly polishing off the cookie jar in one fell swoop.

But let's be honest for a moment. Most of those childhood treats are highly processed and can make you feel like crap. They are usually laden with gluten, dairy, and lots of sugar, which can cause inflammation and a whole host of other issues like brain fog, bloating, and bad skin. The solution is pretty simple, though: skip the gluten, dairy, and refined sugars and come up with recipes that taste just as good! So that's what these are—they are here for when you are craving something sweet but don't want to fall off the wagon. They're full of raw cacao, dates, oats, and fruit—all sweet but unprocessed foods.

Savor decadent salted caramel bonbons at dinner parties, rich spoonfuls of Mexican chocolate pudding for family dessert, blueberry-lime chia pops by the pool, and apple-plum crisp during the changing seasons. These consciously prepared recipes are for anytime, anyplace, all year long.

dragon smoothie bowl

makes 1 large bowl, or 2 snack-size bowls

Dragon fruit, or pitaya, grows from a cactus and gets all the credit for this smoothie bowl's beautiful bold, bright pink hue. Pitaya is high in antioxidants and naturally low in sugar, and pairs well with other fruits—like raspberries and strawberries—because of its relatively mild flavor. Combined with frozen bananas, this bowl has a perfect ice cream–like consistency. An added bonus: The natural sugars from the fruits are balanced with the coconut butter and cinnamon, which help slow down the absorption of sugars. Pile high with your favorite toppings!

ingredients

1 (3.5-ounce/100-g) packet of frozen pitaya

1 banana, cut into chunks and frozen

1 cup (150 g) frozen strawberries

1 cup (240 ml) unsweetened coconut or almond milk (page 48)

1 tablespoon coconut butter

Dash of ground cinnamon

Dash of ground turmeric

Top with: banana, kiwi, strawberry, granola, coconut flakes

method

In a blender, combine the fruits, milk, coconut butter, and spices, and puree until smooth. Pour the smoothie into a bowl and top it with the desired toppings.

tip:
You can purchase pitaya fresh or frozen. It's available in frozen single-serving smoothie packs (which are the most convenient). Aside from smoothies, pitaya is a nice addition to drinks, ice creams, and frozen pops.

goji granola

makes about 6 cups (390 grams)

ingredients

3 cups (270 g)
gluten-free rolled oats

½ cup (50 g) raw
sliced almonds

½ cup (45 g) raw
unsweetened
coconut flakes

½ cup (50 g) raw
pecans, chopped

3 tablespoons
coconut sugar

½ tablespoon
ground cinnamon

½ teaspoon sea salt
or pink salt

¼ cup (60 ml)
coconut oil, melted

⅓ cup (75 ml)
pure maple syrup

1 teaspoon pure
vanilla extract

½ cup (40 g)
goji berries

This recipe is tried and true—it's been made *a lot*, and is super easy to throw together. What really separates this granola from the rest is the big clusters. We all know they're the best part! The trick is to leave the granola alone once you place it in the oven (do not toss!), then let it cool completely before you break it into pieces. Enjoy with any plant-based milk and fruit, on top of your favorite chia pudding, coconut yogurt, or even alone as a snack.

method

Preheat the oven to 350°F (175°C). Line a rimmed baking sheet with parchment paper and set aside.

In a large bowl, combine the oats, almonds, coconut flakes, pecans, coconut sugar, cinnamon, and salt. In a separate bowl, whisk together the coconut oil, maple syrup, and vanilla. Pour the wet mixture over the oats and mix well.

Spread out the granola mixture evenly on the baking sheet and bake for 20 to 25 minutes, or until golden brown. Halfway through, turn the pan around but do not toss the granola.

Let the granola cool completely. Sprinkle the goji berries over it and break it into large clusters. Store the granola in an airtight container on the countertop for up to a month (although it rarely ever lasts more than a week in my apartment!).

go wild for GOJI

Goji berries are one of the most antioxidant-rich foods you can get your hands on. You'll most likely find this small berry, known in Asia as a fountain-of-youth berry, in its sun-dried or powdered form. Beyond boasting a wealth of antioxidants, goji berries are a great source of vitamin A and vitamin C, beta-carotene, iron, and protein. Indigenous to the Himalayas, these nutrient-dense berries were traditionally soaked in hot water and brewed like tea. The berry was said to aid with overall health, vitality, longevity, and youthfulness.

Goji berries look like raisins, but taste more like a mix between a slightly bitter cherry and a slightly sweet tomato. These notes mean gojis can be used in either sweet or savory dishes, making them perfect additions to smoothie bowls, oatmeals, trail mixes, and breakfast bars, but also great in salads or soaked and blended into dressings. Take it traditional by brewing and sipping on goji tea to get your daily dose of free-radical-fighting goodness.

apple-plum crumble

serves 6

There is something special about the late summer months. I love the window of time when these two seasons are bridged and I can continue to squeak out summer-inspired dishes, that also remind us why we love fall so much. When baking, I like to keep the skin on the apples and plums if they are organic. Not only is it easier; but the skins are also full of antioxidants, vitamins, and fiber. The crumble is filled with walnuts and chia seeds, which add a hefty dose of omega-3's. The walnuts also provide the texture and crunch in contrast to the soft, sweet fruit. Serve warm to lots of friends gathered around the table to celebrate fall!

ingredients

fruit filling

2 large apples, chopped

3 or 4 plums, chopped

Juice of ¼ lemon

¼ teaspoon lemon zest

1 tablespoon maple syrup

2 teaspoons arrowroot powder

topping

1 cup (90 g) gluten-free rolled oats

½ cup (45 g) oat flour

½ cup (60 g) walnuts, finely chopped

1 tablespoon chia seeds

¼ teaspoon sea salt or pink salt

¼ cup (50 g) coconut sugar

½ teaspoon ground cinnamon

¼ teaspoon ground nutmeg

2 tablespoons maple syrup

2 tablespoons coconut oil, plus more for the pan

Serve with: coconut yogurt or ice cream

method

Preheat the oven to 350°F (175°C).

For the filling: In a glass or ceramic mixing bowl, combine all the ingredients for the filling, toss well, and set aside.

For the topping: In a separate bowl, combine the oats, flour, walnuts, chia seeds, salt, coconut sugar, cinnamon, and nutmeg, and mix well. Add the maple syrup and coconut oil, and stir until the mixture is well combined.

Grease an 8-inch (20-cm) square baking pan lightly with coconut oil, scoop the filling into the pan, and sprinkle the oat mixture on top in an even layer. Alternatively, divide the apple mixture into 6 individual ramekins (as pictured) and top each with some oat mixture.

Bake the crumble for 35 to 45 minutes, or until cooked through.

Serve with a big dollop of coconut yogurt or your choice of vegan ice cream.

note:
If you prefer to peel the fruit, you'll get a slightly more traditional apple pie–filling texture.

mexican chocolate pudding

serves 4 to 6

ingredients

chocolate pudding

2 cups (480 ml) homemade pumpkin seed milk or almond milk (page 48)

¼ cup plus 2 tablespoons (80 g) chia seeds

¼ cup (20 g) cacao powder, plus more to taste

2 tablespoons maple syrup, plus more to taste

1 teaspoon pure vanilla extract

¼ teaspoon ground cinnamon

¼ teaspoon fine sea salt or pink salt

Small pinch of cayenne

candied pumpkin seeds

½ cup (70 g) pepitas

½ tablespoon maple syrup

Sea salt or pink salt

Top with: candied pumpkin seeds, cacao nibs, and bee pollen

This takes the chocolate pudding of your childhood up a notch. In this recipe, blending the pudding transforms the chia from tapioca-like balls into a velvety pudding-like texture. Beyond the cacao, this dessert is packed with nutrient-rich ingredients, from the omega-rich chia seeds to the magnesium-rich pumpkin seeds. Together, all three ingredients make a dish that will calm your nervous system and lift your mood. Make them fancy, by topping with candied pepitas, cacao nibs, and bee pollen.

method

For the pudding: In a jar, combine the pumpkin seed milk, chia seeds, cacao, maple syrup, vanilla, cinnamon, salt, and cayenne, and shake well. Let sit in the fridge for at least 3 hours or overnight, until a gel-like consistency is achieved.

Transfer the ingredients to a food processor and process until smooth. Taste and add additional sweetener or cacao powder as needed.

For the pumpkin seeds: Heat a heavy-bottomed pan to medium. Add the pepitas and toast, stirring constantly for 2 to 3 minutes. Add the maple syrup and a pinch of salt. Stir until the maple syrup starts to thicken and caramelize, 2 to 3 minutes. Be careful not to burn. Spread the pepitas out on parchment paper and allow to cool.

For serving, give the pudding a good stir and transfer into bowl. Top with candied pumpkin seeds, cacao nibs, and coconut flakes.

Think twice about tossing what you're scooping out of your Halloween pumpkin. Pumpkin seeds—otherwise known as pepitas—are the green seeds held within that white casing. They are an amazing source of fiber, zinc, B vitamins, magnesium, iron, and protein, making them immune-boosting, hormone-balancing, mood-lifting, blood-sugar regulating, and overall inflammation-taming.

Pumpkin seeds have lots of different uses in the kitchen—added to homemade trail mix, sprinkled on salads, candied for desserts, and blended into a mineral-rich milk. You can purchase pumpkin seeds at well-stocked grocers or natural foods stores. Look for seeds that are raw and organic. As with any nut, give them a nice sniff before purchasing to make sure they are good—you'll know if something is off!

salted caramel bonbons

makes 15 to 18 bonbons

When my family moved from California to the East Coast, my grandma started ordering boxes of our favorite California chocolate any occasion she could. By now, my grandma knows all of our favorite chocolates—nuts and chews for my mom and dark caramel patties for me. Old habits die hard. Even without the butter, sugar, and cream, these treats *really* taste like salted caramel, thanks to the creamy almond butter and dates. Next test: sneaking them into the chocolate box and seeing if anyone notices!

ingredients

1 cup (150 g) soft medjool dates, pitted (see Note on page 50)

⅓ cup (75 ml) raw creamy almond butter

1 tablespoon coconut oil, plus more if needed

½ teaspoon sea salt or pink salt, plus more if needed

1 tablespoon almond meal, if needed

1 cup (175 g) dark chocolate chips

Maldon salt, for topping

method

In a food processor, combine the dates, almond butter, coconut oil, and pink salt. Pulse until the mixture is well blended and a ball starts to form. You may need to scrape down the sides a couple of times. Taste and add a pinch more salt as needed, keeping in mind that you will be adding another pinch to top each bonbon.

Pop the large ball of salted caramel "dough" in the freezer to chill for 5 to 10 minutes. If the mixture feels too soft to dip into chocolate and hold its shape, you can freeze it for longer or return it to the food processor and blend in 1 tablespoon almond meal.

Use a small cookie scoop to measure out the bonbons. They should have a flat bottom and round top (like half of a ball). Alternatively, you can use a tablespoon coated in a little coconut oil so the caramel slides out easily. Once they have all been measured out, stick them back in the freezer while you melt the chocolate.

Gently warm the chocolate chips over simmering water in a double boiler (make sure the water does not touch the bowl above it). Stir the chocolate frequently until it is completely melted. Assess the consistency to make sure it will work for dipping; if it's too thick, you can add some melted coconut oil.

When you're ready to dip (this part can get a little bit messy, but it's worth it!), remove the bonbons from the freezer. Line a large plate with parchment. Use 2 forks to gently pick up each bon bon from either side, and carefully roll it around in the chocolate. Set them on the plate and sprinkle each one with a pinch of Maldon salt to finish. Stick them back in the freezer to firm up for about 15 minutes. They'll keep in an airtight container in the fridge for a couple of weeks or in the freezer for a few months.

tip:
If you have leftover chocolate, you can simply pour it onto a parchment-lined baking sheet, sprinkle on your favorite superfood toppings (like hemp hearts, pepitas, goji berries, and bee pollen), and let it set in the fridge or freezer. An easy, delicious treat!

note:
Ideally you will be using fresh, soft dates for this recipe to get the creamiest texture for your caramel. If your medjool dates are not soft, soak them in hot water for a few minutes to soften them.

cookie dough bars

makes 12 small bars

ingredients

3 medjool dates, pitted

¾ cup (90 g) raw cashews

½ cup (45 g) gluten-free rolled oats

½ cup (45 g) unsweetened coconut flakes

¼ teaspoon sea salt or pink salt

1 tablespoon pure vanilla extract

¼ cup (30 g) cacao nibs or dark chocolate chips (45 g)

chocolate sauce (see Note)

¼ cup (20 g) raw cacao powder, plus more as needed

2 tablespoons coconut oil, plus more as needed

1 tablespoon raw honey or maple syrup, plus more as needed

Pinch of sea salt or pink salt

Every time I serve these someone always asks if they can really eat the raw cookie dough. There are no raw eggs—or eggs at all—in them, so you are good to go. They taste like the real deal thanks to the vanilla-date combo, so be sure to use a good vanilla extract. Consider doubling this recipe for a crowd, because these will be the first thing to fly off the dessert table.

method

Place the dates in a small bowl and pour in enough hot water to cover them; let them sit for at least 5 minutes. Line a small pan with parchment and set aside.

To a food processor, add the cashews, oats, coconut flakes, salt, and vanilla and blend until a fine meal forms. If you don't have a food processor, you can use a high-speed blender in its place. Add the dates (make sure there are no pits!), 3 tablespoons of the water the dates have been soaked in, and the vanilla extract. Pulse again until the mixture becomes doughy. Transfer it to a small bowl. Gently fold in the cacao nibs.

Use your hands to evenly press the dough into the pan. Place it in the freezer while you make the chocolate sauce.

Heat a double boiler and add the cacao powder, coconut oil, honey, and salt. Stir and adjust to taste, adding more honey if desired. The chocolate should be runny enough to be drizzled, but not too thin. For a thicker sauce, add more cacao powder; to thin it, add more coconut oil.

Take the pan out of the freezer and drizzle the chocolate sauce over the top. Place the pan back in the freezer and allow the sauce to set for about 20 minutes. Cut it into 12 squares, and enjoy! Store them in the fridge for up to a week or in the freezer for a few months.

note:
The raw chocolate drizzle is beautiful but optional—in fact, if I'm making these for a snack, I will usually roll them into bite-size balls, then roll them in additional unsweetened coconut flakes. Another fun variation is dipping the balls in chocolate. You can also melt dark chocolate over a double boiler in place of making it from scratch.

Cocoa or cacao? This is not your average chocolate! Cacao is where it's at—it contains "happy" chemicals, with mood-lifting, energy-boosting qualities, and is one of the richest sources of antioxidants on the planet, with the same anticancer antioxidants that are found in green tea! It also has a healthy dose of magnesium and iron. I always have raw cacao powder and cacao nibs stocked in my kitchen.

Cacao powder is an amazing alternative to the processed cocoa powders typically used in hot chocolate and sweets. Choose cacao products that are organic and opt for dark chocolate that's at least 70 percent cacao (this means there's less sugar). Stir cacao nibs into cookies and banana bread before baking, or sprinkle them on puddings and ice cream before serving. The slight bitterness from the nibs is reminiscent of the familiar flavor of espresso beans. Chocolate lovers, dig in!

choc-chip cookies

makes 12 to 14 cookies

These chocolate chip cookies are high in protein and are completely grain-free. Both sweet and salty, thanks to the caramel-like flavor of the coconut sugar and the sprinkle of pink salt, they're the perfect everyday cookie to keep in stock at home, or to throw in your bag for a long day of travel. They are super addictive—once you have one, it's pretty hard to stop—make sure to share.

ingredients

1 tablespoon ground flaxseed

1 cup (140 g) raw almonds (or 1¼ cups/ 120 g almond meal)

½ teaspoon sea salt or pink salt

½ teaspoon baking powder

¼ cup (50 g) coconut sugar

¼ cup dark chocolate chips (45 g) or cacao nibs (30 g)

2 tablespoons coconut oil, melted

1 teaspoon pure vanilla extract

method

Preheat the oven to 350°F (175°C). Line a baking sheet with parchment and set aside.

In a small bowl, whisk together the flaxseed with 3 tablespoons of water to form your flax egg. Set it aside for a few minutes or until it forms an egglike consistency.

Add whole almonds, if you're using them, to a food processor and process on high until a fine meal is formed. Be careful not to overprocess them into a butter. Pour the almond meal into a medium-size bowl and add the salt, baking powder, sugar, and chocolate chips.

Once the flax egg has formed, whisk in the coconut oil and vanilla. Pour the mixture into the dry ingredients and stir until just combined. Place the dough in the fridge to chill for at least 30 minutes. This will make it much easier to shape.

Use a tablespoon to scoop out the dough. Roll it into balls and place them on the baking sheet with plenty of space between them, gently pressing them down in the center.

Bake for 10 to 12 minutes, or until the cookies start to turn golden brown but are still soft in the center. Let them cool before removing them from the baking sheet.

Store the cookies in an airtight container for up to 5 days.

double chocolate chews

makes 8 cookies

These are a genius hybrid of a chewy cookie and a gooey brownie, the best of both worlds. The texture will vary depending on what type of nut butter you use and its consistency. If you are using a creamy natural almond butter, you will get a thinner cookie, whereas a "bottom-of-the-almond-butter-jar" cookie will be thicker. A quick tip for when you get your almond butter: Store it upside down so the oil distributes evenly and give it a nice stir before using.

ingredients

½ cup (90 g) dark chocolate chips

½ cup (120 ml) raw almond butter

1 pasture-raised egg

2 tablespoons maple syrup

2 tablespoons unsweetened almond milk (page 48)

1 teaspoon pure vanilla extract

½ teaspoon fine pink salt

½ teaspoon baking powder

1 tablespoon cacao nibs (optional)

Maldon salt, for topping

method

Preheat the oven to 350°F (175°C). Line a baking sheet with parchment and set aside.

Gently warm half of the chocolate chips over simmering water in a double boiler until melted. Add the melted chocolate to a food processor with the almond butter, egg, maple syrup, almond milk, vanilla extract, salt, and baking powder. Pulse until well combined. You can also use a handheld mixer instead. Stir in the remaining chocolate chips and the cacao nibs, if you're using them.

At this point you should have a sticky, wet batter that looks like very thick almond butter. It won't resemble your average cookie dough—don't worry! Use a spoon to scoop large dollops of it onto the baking sheet (the cookies should be about 3 inches/7.5 cm in diameter).

Bake the cookies for 10 to 12 minutes, until they are slightly golden on the bottom and look slightly puffed up. Let them cool for 5 minutes and then, using a spatula, transfer them to a wire rack. Allow to cool for at least another 10 minutes. Resist the urge to dig in—I promise they will be much tastier once cooled!

cherry-coco ice cream sandwich

makes 4 full-size sandwiches

ingredients

cherry coconut ice cream

1 (15-ounce/450-ml) can coconut milk

1 cup (120 g) cashews, soaked overnight

2 cups (520 g) frozen cherries

2 to 4 tablespoons (30 to 60 ml) maple syrup

1 teaspoon pure vanilla extract

1 teaspoon fresh lemon juice

Pinch of sea salt or pink salt

2 tablespoons cacao nibs

ice cream sandwiches

Double chocolate chews (page 194)

Unsweetened coconut flakes, for rolling

The cherry-and-chocolate combo is one of my all-time favorites, and ice cream sandwiches are the perfect vehicle for these flavors. Good news: You don't even need an ice cream maker for this recipe! The cherry coconut–cashew ice cream base turns out perfectly creamy with a blender, and makes about 1 quart (960 ml), so you'll have some left over. I've found that a solid ice cream sandwich cookie is tough to get right, but my double chocolate chews stand the test.

method

Line a loaf pan with parchment and set aside.

For the ice cream: In a blender, combine the milk, cashews, cherries, 2 tablespoons of the maple syrup, the vanilla, lemon, and salt and blend until smooth. Taste and adjust the maple syrup as needed. Keep in mind that the ice cream will be slightly less sweet once it's frozen. Add the cacao nibs and blend briefly to break up the pieces a bit more.

Pour the mixture into the loaf pan and place it in the freezer for at least 4 hours, or until frozen. Stir it every 30 minutes to help create a creamy consistency. Once it's frozen, remove from the freezer and let sit for 5 to 10 minutes to soften.

Assemble the sandwiches: Put a nice scoop of ice cream between two of the cookies and gently press them together. Roll the sides in the coconut flakes. Enjoy immediately.

crazy for COCONUTS

Coconuts are among the most versatile foods on the planet—from coconut water to coconut oil to coconut meat, there are a wide range of uses and products all derived from the same source. Coconuts are fruits or, more specifically, drupes. Coconut oil is antibacterial and antifungal, making it a good line of defense against bacteria and viruses that cause flus and common colds, and against other issues like candida overgrowth. It's also high in healthy fats known as medium-chain triglycerides (MCTs), which can help regulate weight and boost metabolism.

This inflammation-taming, detoxifying, and cholesterol-balancing fruit has a strong place in the kitchen *and* the bathroom. Coconut oil is stable at high temperatures so it's one of my favorite oils for cooking. Use coconut water as a delicious, natural electrolyte in smoothies or frozen pops (page 124 and 198), coconut butter blended into dreamy lattes, and coconut flakes for topping smoothie bowls and ice cream sandwiches. Use the jar in your bathroom for oil pulling (page 58) or as a makeup remover, moisturizer, or shaving cream.

blueberry-lime chia pops

makes 6 to 8 pops

This pop is an upgrade to the standard strawberry shortcake ice cream bar I used to get as a kid. Blueberries are made refreshing when paired with lime, and the coconut water also makes this a hydrating treat on a warm day. Don't go overboard with the chia seeds, though. Too many will turn the mixture into a consistency that won't fully harden up in the molds. You can substitute other summer berries like strawberries or raspberries for the blueberries if you'd like!

ingredients

½ tablespoon chia seeds

½ cup (120 ml) coconut water

1 cup (145 g) blueberries

½ cup (120 ml) coconut milk

1 teaspoon coconut

Juice of 1 lime

2 to 3 tablespoons raw honey

¼ teaspoon lime zest

method

In a small jar, combine the chia seeds and coconut water. Stir well and let thicken for about an hour, until the seeds have expanded.

In a blender, combine the blueberries, coconut milk, oil, lime juice, and honey; puree until smooth. Strain the mixture into a bowl, and stir in the chia seed mixture and lime zest. Pour or spoon the mixture into 3-ounce (90 ml) molds and let it freeze for 8 hours or overnight.

Let the pops sit at room temperature for a few minutes before removing them from the molds. Wrap them individually in plastic and store them in the freezer for up to 2 months.

raw apple cider vinegar

spirulina

hydrating
coco-avo
face mask

raw cacao powder

avocado

hydrating coco-avo face mask

makes 2 face masks

This face mask was born in my kitchen after a long day in the sun, but it's equally a remedy for dry winter skin. Spirulina has more antioxidants than blueberries, calms inflammation, and helps repair skin from sun or dirty-air damage. The best thing to do is to stay protected when you are in the sun and wear proper protection when you're outside, but a weekly dose of antioxidants on the face will help your cause either way. This mask, with its combination of avocado, cacao powder, and raw apple cider vinegar, is pore-shrinking and clarifying, while also hydrating and softening.

AVOCADO
is anti-inflammatory and keeps skin moisturized and hydrated.

RAW CACAO POWDER
is rich in antioxidants, contains caffeine, and fights free-radical damage to the skin.

RAW APPLE CIDER VINEGAR
is antibacterial and antifungal, fighting acne and dark spots on the skin.

SPIRULINA
is antibacterial, cleansing, and clarifying, and also protects skin cells from stress.

ingredients

¼ avocado

1 teaspoon raw cacao powder

½ teaspoon raw apple cider vinegar

¼ teaspoon spirulina

method

In a small bowl, whip all ingredients together with a fork until well combined. Apply to face for 10 minutes, then rinse well with warm water. Store remaining mask in the fridge, tightly covered, for a day.

parties

now that you have new recipes to try, it's time to get cooking (and partying)! It goes without saying that good food is made even better when you're surrounded by great friends and people you love. It doesn't matter if you have a big dining room table or are gathered around a coffee table with a hodge podge of chairs like my early days in New York. These simple spreads have been tried and true in the smallest of kitchens but the results are always the same: happy friends and family. Here are a few of my favorite parties, feel free to put your own together from other recipes in this book.

smoothie bowl breakfast

bottomless brunch

mexi-cali breakfast bowls (page 80)
mini carrot gingerbread muffins (page 170)
super green smoothie (page 105)

ladies' lunch

curry date night
red lentil earth curry (page 140)
steamed vegetables (page 30)
sunny immunity bowl (page 130)

dinner with friends

sesame noodle bowls with
  pan-fried tofu (page 94)
simple slaw (page 41)
smashed cucumbers (page 40)

acknowledgments

I never imagined that sharing photos of what I cook on social media would turn into writing a cookbook only a couple years later. I can't express how grateful I am for my dedicated followers and blog readers for your kind emails and comments. You always make my day.

This book was a labor of love and I couldn't have done it without my amazing team. Thank you to:

My photographers, Gemma and Andy Ingalls, for creating beautiful photographs and being great company on set. I miss our afternoon matchas!

My aunt, Carol Cotner Thompson, chef and food stylist, for assisting treacherously long (but fun!) days on set and helping to make the food look beautiful. You have been an amazing mentor along the way.

Both of my sisters: Rachel, for so generously allowing the *Good Clean Food* team to invade your home for the photo shoot, and for letting me cook until midnight and wake up as the sun rose to start again. And Katie, for your dedication to recipe testing and meticulous attention to detail; I can ask you just about any question related to cooking.

Lucia Litman, for your dedication, for always believing in CFDC, and for being a reliable sounding board. If flying down to LA with a concussion isn't dedication, I don't know what is!

All of my amazing family and friends: My parents, for believing in me when I told them I was quitting my day job to write a cookbook. My best friends, for giving me my first set of white dinnerware to shoot on. Justine—I cannot imagine navigating the last few years without you by my side, or without choc-chip cookies tucked in our bags! My roomies, Sophia and Elisabeth, for living with me through months of writing and recipe testing for a book, but most importantly for your feedback on the recipes.

The rest of my wonderful recipe testers: Mom, Irina, Justine, Erica, Kendra, and Reva. And many more friends whose trusted advice and ideas helped me along the way.

The entire team at Abrams: My editor, Sarah Massey, who followed my blog and Instagram, and had an understanding from the beginning of what *Good Clean Food* could be. Your dedication and love for clean food (including recipe testing!) is much appreciated. My designer, Deb Wood, who put together this beautiful, clean book that is beyond my dreams. Thank you to Holly Dolce, Mary Hern, Denise LaCongo, Ana Deboo, Jane Bobko, and Sarah Scheffel.

My amazing agent, Alison Fargis, for your support and guidance and seeing a vision of this book from the beginning.

Last but certainly not least, thank you to my four-legged friend Pucci, for being my sous chef every long day in the kitchen and cleaning up everything I dropped. If only she could do dishes!

And to the city that never sleeps: Thank you for providing me with endless amounts of inspiration and farmer's market produce. Your cramped kitchens foster creativity and made Clean Food Dirty City what it is today!

Index

Editor: Sarah Massey
Designer: Deb Wood
Production Manager: Denise LaCongo

Library of Congress Control Number: 2016940434

ISBN: 978-1-4197-2390-2

Printed and bound in the United States
10 9 8 7 6 5 4 3 2 1

Abrams books are available at special discounts
when purchased in quantity for premiums and
promotions as well as fundraising or educational
use. Special editions can also be created to specifi-
cation. For details, contact specialsales@
abramsbooks.com or the address below.

ABRAMS The Art of Books
115 West 18th Street, New York, NY 10011
abramsbooks.com